To Don
All the best
Laffit Pincay Jr.

LAFFIT

ANATOMY OF A WINNER

THE BIOGRAPHY OF LAFFIT PINCAY JR.

BY MADELYN CAIN

All the best,
Madelyn Cain

A

AFFIRMED PRESS, PASADENA, CA.

ISBN: 978-0-615-23821-0
Library of Congress Control Number: 2008906976
All rights reserved.

Published by Affirmed Press
Copyright @ 2008 Madelyn Cain

First printing
Printed in the United States

Cover Design by: Daniel Will-Harris, www.will-harris.com
Cover photo by: Benoit Photo

www.affirmedpress.com

Affirmed Press
650 Sierra Madre Villa Avenue
Pasadena, CA 91107

Acknowledgements

No book springs to life without the encouragement of many people. This book, and this author, are certainly indebted to many individuals.

Foremost among those to be thanked is Michael Bello. This book was his idea and it was he who brought Laffit and myself together (a very happy occurrence for me.) Michael provided the initial support to get the book off the ground.

Along the way, a variety of people provided much needed information. Mike Mooney, the publicist at Hollywood Park Racetrack, offered generous help with statistics and horse racing history. Mike never said no and always gave more than was asked for. This book is indebted to his generosity.

A thanks to Rayetta and the folks at Benoit Photography who allowed me to pick through their very excellent photo collection. Many of the photos included in this book, including the jacket photo, are courtesy of them. And a special thanks to Steve Schuelein who graciously provided racing terminology and data.

Jill Marsal, my agent at Sandra Dykstra Literary Agency, was as supportive of this book as any agent could be. I feel lucky to have her in my corner.

I am particularly indebted to Christopher Meeks who was unsparing in his guidance and to Gina Nahai who offered help and encouragement along the way. A thanks to those in the Master of Professional Writing Program at USC who inspire me, both students and faculty alike.

Those who were interviewed all shared a common goal: to get the story right. I hope I have not disappointed any of them, most particularly Laffit's daughter Lisa, and sons Laffit III and Jean-Laffit.

The challenge of writing a biography is that some facts, some incidents, and in this case, some races, will not be touched upon. Other events will be remembered by various parties in different ways. I have done my best to gather as much verifiable and objective information as possible, but realize that not everything will feel complete to some people. I offer my apologies in advance to those who wanted what was not included here.

Perhaps the person most invested in seeing Laffit's story told is his friend, Tom Kessler. Michael Bello was the inspiration, Tom Kessler was the maestro who brought the book to its final presentation. Kudos to Tom.

To my family – Paul, Elizabeth, Julie, Catherine and Mike, thank you for making my life so rich and for keeping me balanced.

And finally, a thank you to Laffit. From the beginning, Laffit was committed to telling the whole story. If anything speaks of healthy self-assurance, it has been his willingness to unabashedly share his incredible life with me, and now with you. I thank him for trusting me with his remarkable story.

Madelyn Cain

Contents

PRELUDE

Laffit as a baby.

"Quickly, come quickly, Laffit, they're about to start," his mother calls excitedly. Rosario turns and extends her hand down to her son. The incline behind Presidente Remón racetrack is steep for a four-year-old but his mother easily lifts him with a sharp yank and brings him to the top of the dirt mound, and to the wide, white fence on the back end of the racetrack. The young boy jumps his sandaled feet onto the bottom of the wooden rail and hooks his slender, tanned arms around the top. His mother stands behind him, her arms wrapped around his chest and whispers in his ear, "Look to your right, niño, that's where they'll start." She points and his eyes follow.

There is a sound in the distance and the horses burst forward, moving away from where young Laffit stands. Within seconds, however, they are parallel with him and the picture is clearer. In the distance he sees animals racing with abandon, their long necks strained, fighting for position. They are ridden by men in blazing colors, some of whom he notices are whipping the horses' flanks.

His eyes are focused on the chestnut horse in front, the one with the rider in green. As the horses and riders round the turn toward him, he can feel the earth under him begin to shake as the thundering of the hooves grows louder. His heart races with excitement. The man in green approaches.

Then it happens. The chestnut horse buckles and when it does, the picture abruptly changes—the earth smokes, clouding the air. Horses' legs flail, and bodies in bright colors drift through the dusty sky only to tumble back down onto the red clay below. The boy holds his breath.

Finally, the dust abates. Those horses not caught in the wreck come trampling toward him and go by in a flash, intent on finishing—on winning. But he does not keep his eyes on those still in the race. Instead, he looks to see the broken clump trying to right itself. An ambulance can be heard moving toward the pileup.

Three jockeys remain on the ground. One horse stands, another lays on its side. The chestnut horse lifts its head and gingerly gets up. The jockey wearing green, the object of his intense curiosity, slowly gets back on his horse.

Now the child is anxious to see this horse as it makes its way toward him. He wants to touch it. The horse ambles his way, walking as if his legs were wrapped in wet cement. Laffit observes the jockey wince each time the horse's gait drops downward.

For the first time he notices that the green shirt has white stripes, too, and that the jockeys' satin helmet is covered in grime. The rider's leather boots, more luxurious than any he has ever seen, have deep creases across the ankles and they, too, are caked with dirt. Stirrups from the saddle dangle on the sides of the horse, torn loose, mangled in the fall. The broken rider has nowhere to put his feet. His legs lay listlessly against the sides of the horse.

As he passes in front of where the young boy stands, the jockey looks down at the young Laffit. He does not smile, he does not frown, but looks penetratingly into the eyes of the child. There is no fear in the man's eyes, no apology for what has happened. This is his business, his eyes tell the boy, and he endures it with pride.

This is not a jockey passing his way who has lost a race, nor a mere athlete, the boy understands. This man is a hero, a warrior in a saddle.

And at that moment, ambition is born.

Panama

Chapter 1

The man took the cigar out of his mouth and ground it into the red earth of the barn.

"Okay kid, you can work here but remember, you have to be on time, 6:00 AM, seven days a week, rain or shine. Skip a day and you're out. You want to be a jockey, you have to work. You want to work, you work for free. If you work hard, maybe one day I'll let you exercise the horses. You can start by cleaning out the stables—there's a pitchfork on that wall." He pointed to the last stall. "Chati will tell you where everything is."

The man turned to leave with one parting comment. "You're very lucky I'm letting somebody so green have a shot."

I made it! He thought. *I got the job*!

Now he had to tell his mother.

Getting his mother to agree to his plan had not been easy. Rosario fought her son for weeks. Luckily, Laffit's stepfather understood the boy's needs and guided his wife.

"You can't hold him back, Rosario. This is what he wants to do," Juan advised. "You have to let him."

Fear gripped Rosario, *What if he isn't good at racing? What if he gets injured? What will happen to him then?* She knew all about the racing world. Her brother was a jockey and Laffit's father, her ex-husband, was one too. She had nursed the broken bones, the cracked ribs, the sprained ankles. She knew the risks first-hand—risks her rambunctious fifteen year-old couldn't fathom in his overwhelming enthusiasm.

She would say yes *only* if he went to school to learn bookkeeping. Laffit would

Laffit's childhood home. Their apartment was the lower one on the corner.

rise at 4:30 AM to get to the barn, leave there at 10 AM to catch the bus to school and take classes until six o'clock. He would then go home, eat, do his homework and sleep.

He couldn't wait to begin.

On his first day on the job, Laffit came face to face with a horse that was tall and intimidating and shook his head every time the young man approached, rebuffing him with his eyes. Disgusted by the boy's trepidations he finally snorted, turning his head away. He had no time for amateurs.

"Don't jump back like that." Chati instructed the newcomer. "He senses you're afraid of him."

Laffit was terrified, something he didn't dare tell Chati How could he fulfill his dream of being a jockey if he didn't conquer this unanticipated, overpowering fear of horses?

"Put your hand under the horse's nose like this. Let him smell you."

The young man did so, worried the horse might bite off his hand. He had shown his teeth earlier. They were dark brown and powerful.

The horse sniffed the boy's hand and then his arm. His face was now inches from Laffit's. He could feel the breath on his bare skin and the moisture emanating from the horse's nose. Laffit worked to slow his beating heart. *I can do this*, he told himself.

"Good. Now put your left hand on his nose and keep it there for a minute. Look the horse in the eyes." The horse was gigantic with eyes the size of saucers. Laffit hoped the man didn't notice his shaking legs as he willed them to stop. "Keep your hand on the horse's nose, and move slowly to his left side. No, the *left* side. Good. Now pat the horse." Laffit patted the shimmering black coat. The horse was shaking his head. He suddenly seemed happy.

"Are you ready to mount him?" Chati asked. Laffit nodded yes though every instinct cried no.

"Here, put your leg in my hands and I'll help you up."

He put his dusty shoe in Chati's cupped hands and with a swift lift Laffit was in the saddle. The height made him dizzy. He was so high up he thought he might be sick.

A noisy car drove by the barn and the horse jumped back.

"Don't kick him! He'll think you want him to run." But it was too late. The horse reared up.

"Grab hold of the reins and his mane! Don't let go."

Adrenaline was pumping through the young man and through the horse. Laffit saw the veins in the horse's neck grow pronounced and felt those on his own neck ready to explode. The groom stepped in and grabbed the rein, telling the horse, "Whoa, whoa."

Finally, the horse calmed. The moment he did, Laffit jumped off, scurried to the side of the stable and slid down the wall, putting his head on his knees.

"You okay?" Chati asked.

A choked voice came out. "I'll be fine. I just need a minute."

"You can try again tomorrow."

"No." Laffit said, lifting his head and shaking it. "I'm getting back on."

The terrified boy moved back and gripped both the rein and the mane. This horse would not keep him from his goal. Another assist and he was back on the horse. He was steadier this time.

"I'll ride him around the barn," Laffit told the surprised Chati. He guided the now obedient horse out the open door. Though fear still slept within his soul, at that moment determination triumphed. He conquered the horse, and his fear, that day.

To endure the backbreaking work of the barn, Laffit clung to his dream of riding. The highlight of his week was the day he spent in jockey school and it was here that he focused all his attention.

Jockey school was conducted in a dusty room tucked behind the stables. The group, eight boys in all, met each week for an hour and learned the ropes, literally.

"I want each of you to get on top of a barrel," Bolivar Moreno's booming voice instructed his class on the very first day. "Mount your barrel and grab hold of the ropes on each side." The novice riders did as they were instructed, delighted to be taught by a talented jockey they respected. Moreno was the only teacher, and he was a good one.

"Those are your reins. You will control the horse with your feet in the stirrups and your hands on the reins."

Moreno circulated the room and started with the basics.

"The reins are how you will speak to the horse in a language he understands. Wrap the reins around your hands. No, Hector, don't trap your thumb like that. You need to have it free. " His teaching was practical, straightforward. Each class concentrated on a particular skill that Moreno wanted his students to master.

With each class Laffit seemed to be the first to develop the grip, the stance, the extended arm push. After class Moreno would comment to Laffit that he knew he was going to be a great rider one day.

But after a few months, riding a barrel grew frustrating for the hopeful young jockey. He wanted to be on a real horse.

The stalls on the north end of the barn, where Laffit worked, housed a friendly group of people. They traded tips, secrets, frustrations … and hope.

Reginald Douglas was the trainer whose stalls were directly across from where Laffit worked and with whom Laffit had a comfortable rapport. One day Douglas yelled to him,

"You think you can handle Sheba?"

"Sure I do." Laffit replied, brushing a grey mare.

"Maybe you can take her out on the track."

Laffit stopped what he was doing and turned to Douglas. "The track? You mean it? When?"

"Today. Now."

"Really?"

"Yeah, why not? Just don't go crazy out there. Let her gallop a little. Ride her short."

"Yes, sir."

An excited Laffit quickly saddled Sheba before Douglas could change his mind. He was desperate to ride. In the past few months his old fear of horses had turned to lust.

A trainer was letting him ride! He couldn't believe his luck. He slowly walked the horse out of the barn. It was mid-afternoon and few people were on the track.

He mounted the horse and what had been a dizzying height the first time now felt like a majestic throne. Before he let the horse step onto the turf though, Laffit stopped. He knew this was a solemn moment and he said a silent prayer.

I don't know if I'm ever gonna make it as a jockey but I promise, I solemnly promise, that I am going to do the very best that I can every time I ride, so help me God.

With that he nudged the horse gently, as he'd practiced doing on a barrel, and was on the track for the very first time.

Laffit's heart swelled with joy. He kicked the horse to start him galloping. He resisted the urge to look at the few other riders on the track. Though he momentarily worried that his style might reveal he was a beginner, his focus quickly shifted to Sheba and keeping the horse in line. He knew Douglas would be watching from the sidelines and he wanted the trainer to see he was able to control the horse.

The smell of the track, the powerful animal beneath him—obeying his commands—filled Laffit with an emotion he'd never known before. One jockey passed him and nodded hello—treated him like an equal! The sun washed his face and the wind whipped it clean. He felt reborn, as though he had come to a place he'd always been searching for, a place his soul desperately needed. He was home, and he knew it in the depth of his being.

One morning one of the nearby trainers offered Laffit the chance to jog his horse, Batistin. Jogging was a huge step for the novice jockey and as many jockeys did, Laffit rode bareback that day.

Laffit gave Batistin the gentle signal to jog but the horse, clearly with a mind of its own, took off at a gallop. Laffit grabbed the reins tightly, pulling with all this might, but Batistin moved with lightning speed. He pressed in his knees, but without the stirrups his feet had no traction. He pulled on the mane. There was no reaction from the horse whatsoever. He pulled on the reins again. Nothing. This horse was unstoppable. He remembered something he'd been taught in jockey school and lifted the horse's head as high as he could. Still, no reaction. They whizzed by other jockeys who yelled out "Slow down, slow down!" which caused the initial fear that had been put to rest inside Laffit a year earlier to resurface stronger than ever.

He did not have control of the horse, and with each turn Batistin was quickening the pace. Without stirrups and a saddle, the young jockey was slipping this way and that. *My mother was right*, he lamented to himself, *I should be in school!* Not only was the horse not slowing down, he seemed to be gaining speed!

Laffit wasn't afraid of a spill—he'd accepted that as part of being a jockey—but on this ride he feared being paralyzed or maybe even killed, of his dreams ending right on this track, this day, before he'd ever ridden in his first race. Tears began to form in Laffit's eyes.

Finally, and only because the horse grew tired of the game, Batistin slowed down to a reasonable pace and allowed Laffit to guide him back to the barn.

"What happened?" the trainer demanded when the sweaty horse and rider got back to the barn." I told you to jog the horse, not run him into the ground."

Laffit feared the man would end his career right there. But there was no point in lying. The man had witnessed the whole thing.

"The horse just took off," he confessed, "I couldn't control him."

The man tilted his head and smiled at the young jockey.

"Don't look so glum. You'll learn."

And he did. Laffit could be seen on the track daily galloping, trotting, and walking horses, incorporating the lessons he was learning in jockey school.

"You're doing a good job out there, boy. You keep that up and you'll be wearing silks one day soon." It was the kind of encouragement Laffit began to hear and every word spurred him on.

The more skilled he became, however, the more frustrated Laffit grew.

"Mr. Moreno, you *have* to give me my license," he pleaded to his instructor. "I can't get a mount unless I have it."

"What is your rush? Laffit, I told you, you're going to be a great jockey someday. I've watched you out there."

"Then you know I can do it."

"Be patient, boy."

But Laffit was not patient. In fact, he was desperate. After months of pleading, Moreno relented and finally signed the license that would allow Laffit to ride his first race. All Laffit had to do now was find a mount.

The following Monday the program listing the weekend's races was distributed. Like other hopefuls, jockey agents, and seasoned jocks, Laffit began the trek from barn to barn to sweet-talk trainers.

"I was wondering, Mr. Jeronimo, if you had committed your horse already for Friday's fifth race?"

"Sorry, kid, I promised Eduardo that ride."

"What about the third race on Sunday?"

"Come back when you've got a little experience."

"I'm really good."

"How many races have you won?"

He tried to not let the rejections sink his hopes.

Then one day, it happened.

"How much do you weigh?"

Laffit feared the question was a trap. "What are you looking for?

"I need a really light jockey for this horse."

How much to tell the man was Laffit's biggest concern. He weighed 106 pounds.

"103."

"Can you make 100 pounds by Saturday?"

"Absolutely."

"This your first race?"

Laffit smiled. "You got me."

The smile was not returned. "Three dollars, that's the pay."

Regular jockeys were getting five dollars per race.

"That's fine."

Finally, a smile from the man. "Kid, you've got yourself a race."

Laffit wanted to jump for joy but knew he had to act like a professional.

"I'll see you on Saturday then," he told the trainer and left to jog off six pounds.

Laffit couldn't wait to get home to share the good news.

"I got my first race, Mama. I'm riding on Saturday on a horse called Huelen!"

With that, his mother began to cry.

The neighborhood was abuzz. Laffit was riding in his first race! Cesar, his sister Margie's new husband, filled his car with as many people as he could and transported the group to the racetrack.

People from the neighborhood shouted to those in the car.

"Good luck."

"We know he's going to win."

"Here," a neighbor ran up to them with money. "Bet this on Laffit."

Everyone on his street was thrilled to see Laffit fulfill his dream. Everyone that is, except Rosario. Whereas Laffit had conquered his fears, Rosario's were just beginning. The news that he had secured his first mount put a permanent lump in her throat. It was such a dangerous sport. She prayed all week long that her son would be safe.

Young jockeys need boots and pants—both would have to be custom-made … and quickly. Rosario, despite her trepidations, dipped into her savings and had the items specially made for her son. How could she not?

That week before his first ride, Laffit refused to eat, no matter how much his mother told him he needed his strength to ride.

"I know what I'm doing," was all he said when she pleaded with him.

The morning of the race, Rosario hugged her firstborn and whispered in his ear, "Good luck, niño."

"Thank you, Mama."

"Do me a favor."

"What is it?"

"Wear your underpants inside out today."

He pulled back from her. "Why?" He laughed, looking in her eyes.

"To ward off any evil spirits."

He smiled, giving her a kiss.

"Don't laugh," she told him. "It works."

The car arrived at Hipódromo Presidente Remón Racetrack on March 22, 1964, and the cramped, excited troop piled out. They placed their bets and were in the stands waiting for the eighth race to begin, joking about what they would do with their winnings. All, that is, but Rosario. She sat silently twisting the hanky in her hands.

Laffit walked into the jockeys' room both excited and apprehensive. He'd been there many times before when he sneaked in to weigh himself on the official scale, but today he officially belonged.

That afternoon he weighed in at exactly 100 lbs. Starving himself and jogging countless miles had been worth it. In five days, he'd lost the six pounds.

Jockeys, some in silks, some half-naked, were scattered around the room. He searched the small cubicles and found an empty one in the back and laid out his few things.

"First race?" The man next to him inquired.

"Yeah. How did you know?"

"New boots and pants." The man smiled at him.

"Welcome."

"Thank you."

The valet brought him the red and yellow silks. He slipped them over his head and looked into the tiny mirror he'd brought from home. He smiled at himself. He looked like a jockey.

He waited for the seventh race to end, sitting on a bench in the middle of the room. He nodded to one of the jockeys he sometimes walked the track with in the morning.

"Good luck today," the man yelled.

"Thank you."

"Nervous?"

"A little."

"You'll do fine. I've seen you out there."

When the announcer called the eighth race, Laffit began to head out.

"Hey Laffit," his new friend called, "where's your helmet?"

"Oh, I must have forgotten it," he lied.

"Looks like you forgot your crop, too. Here, borrow these."

The man walked over and handed them to Laffit, leaning in to whisper some advice.

"Don't let them keep you on the outside," he said.

"Thanks." Laffit looked into the man's friendly eyes, gratefully took the items, and headed to the paddock.

The groomsman led Huelen into the gate easily. Laffit's stomach was doing summersaults. In the stands, his family was equally nervous. Laffit instructed the horse boy:

"Get his nose right up to the gate. Hold him there."

When the announcer blared that the horses were in the gate, the fear became too much for Rosario. She whispered to her husband that she would be in the ladies' room and quickly scurried off.

Once the gate snapped open, Laffit's focus was razor sharp. Though he knew the horse was not expected to win, he would ride him for all he was worth. He began as he'd planned, at the back of the pack and slowly moved up and through the crowd of horses. The horse was following his commands, he was happy to see, and had more fire in him than he'd expected. Another turn and Laffit made his move. Suddenly he was near the front, with just two other horses ahead of him. His heart began to leap. *Could it be*, he wondered? They rode apace for a while, but then the two horses in front stretched out their lead, two, three, five lengths. Huelen tried holding his own, but Laffit could feel him beginning to deflate. He whipped him on the right and the horse gave a valiant push but Huelen was too tired and the other horses were now seven lengths beyond his reach, eight. It was clear now he was going to come in dead last.

It was over too soon. Laffit wanted to do it again. He knew he could do better.

He lay awake that night replaying the race in his head searching for clues as to what he could have done to improve the outcome.

The trainer of the horse, however, was pleased with the race. Pleased enough that he told Laffit he would let him ride Huelen the following week.

That week Laffit prepared even harder, mentally planning the race as it would unfold with every detail predetermined, including crossing the finish line in first place. It didn't matter that Huelen was a long shot.

The following week, March 28th, five horses ran. Huelen was the longest shot on the board. The break from the gate was good, but this time he didn't want to wear the horse down too soon. He would need a burst of energy during that final stretch. It was dark by the time the race began and the lights at the track went on just as they came to the second pole.

Another horse moved strongly ahead and took the lead. Laffit freed his horse ever so slightly and let him take to the middle of the pack. When he felt the time was right, Laffit released Huelen. The horse had been frustrated being held back and he responded as he'd hoped. He quickly took the lead. The sudden speed felt good but the helmet he'd borrowed was so large it floated around his head. Not wanting any distraction Laffit whipped the helmet off mid-race and threw it over the fence.

They rounded the last turn toward the finish line and Huelen was neck and neck with another horse. Laffit concentrated on controlling his horse but in the back of his mind, the thought was taking hold. *Victory was possible.* He gave the horse another swish from the crop, pushed the horse's neck out and forward with all his strength, and unbelievably, unbelievably, Huelen crossed the finish line the winner.

The roar from the crowd was enormous—a new jockey riding a long shot had just won! Laffit was ecstatic. His heart pumped wildly within his chest. His dream had become reality. He raised himself up on the horse so that he was practically standing to slow Huelen down. His mind felt as though fireworks were going off inside. He would savor this moment, so much had gone into it.

Laffit on Huelen after his first win.

They led Huelen to the winner's circle to take the victory picture. Someone scrambled to the ladies' room to quickly fetch his mother. Finally, when they were all assembled, the photo was taken and history was recorded.

"Laffit, you know what that horse paid?" His friend Blass shouted up to Laffit sitting in the saddle. "Twenty-six to one!" They had each placed a two-dollar bet and now felt wealthy beyond measure.

Laffit dismounted and hugged his mother, whispering in her ear, "Mama, I turned my underpants inside out."

His mother beamed. She didn't have to say, "I told you so." It was in her eyes.

Laffit's first winning purse netted him forty dollars. He gave ten dollars to his mother, took ten for himself and instructed his mother to put the other twenty dollars in the bank.

That night the winning jockey couldn't sleep. He replayed the race over and over in his mind—the nervousness at the beginning, the calm when the race began, the mounting excitement as the horse did what he'd hoped and finally, the elation of crossing the finish line, standing in the stirrups to slow the horse down, his right arm held high in the air in a victory salute. The experience was even better than he'd dreamed it would be.

The following week, he and his jockey cousin went from stable to stable seeking another mount.

"You should ride that horse," Laffit told Hector, pointing at Imperialista.

"Are you crazy? That horse has no tail. I would never ride a horse without a tail."

Laffit met the tailless horse's trainer and asked to ride him.

"Afraid I've already got someone for that horse."

"Oh, well, thanks anyway."

Laffit turned to leave.

"Can you make the weight?" The man suddenly asked.

Laffit turned back.

"Sure I can." He hoped he didn't sound too eager.

When the man said nothing further, Laffit turned and began to walk away.

"Hey kid, come back." The man's head was cocked as though he was contemplating something.

"No, you ride him. Here." The man signed the slip for the racing secretary.

"Give this to Mola. Tell him that I'm giving you that mount."

"Yes, sir!"

On the day of the race, odds on Imperialista were that the horse would come in dead last. He didn't. Thanks to Laffit's riding—and everyone that day saw it was the rider, not the horse, that had triumphed that afternoon—Imperialista came in a very close second. Though it wasn't a win, it was a major victory. Laffit may have still have been an apprentice, but he was now seen as a professional.

Racing at Presidente Remon Racetrack. Laffit is in front.

From then on, trainers were coming to Laffit asking him to ride their horses.

Within a month, he went from no mounts to four mounts a day. The money, and the recognition, began flowing in.

Meanwhile, that original ten-dollar winning money stayed in Laffit's back pocket. He was too busy to spend it.

CHANGES

CHAPTER 2

The ride on Imperialista was the turning point. Some began calling Laffit the next Braulio Baeza, and everyone in Panama knew what had happened to Baeza when Ramone Navarro, the manager of the racetrack, took notice. Navarro called Fred Hooper, a wealthy horse owner. If Hooper liked a particular rider, he would put him under contract and arrange for U.S. residency papers. Friends and family members often bragged about the fancy cars these jockeys owned and the mansions they lived in. Such stories of success in America tantalized every young jockey who rode in Panama. Laffit was no exception.

"Mama, Mr. Navarro brought me home today. He said he wants to talk to us."

"He is here?"

"Si. He's outside in his car."

"What does he want to talk about?"

"I don't know. Should I show him in?"

Rosario took off her apron. "Don't leave the man outside."

Laffit ran to fetch Mr. Navarro.

An early interview. The crop was a gift sent from his father in Venezuela.

The last two years in Panama had been exciting. Of all his mounts, 1,401, Laffit had won almost a third of them—449 races. He placed second and third in another 514 races,[1] an astonishing number for any rider, let alone a teenaged beginner. There was little doubt that Laffit was a jockey on the rise.

Laffit suspected/hoped/prayed that Navarro was coming to talk to them about Fred Hooper. If he was lucky, and Hooper was interested, his mother's permission would be necessary before he could go anywhere. He told Laffit he wanted to talk to his mother *too*. It had to be something important, Laffit reasoned.

Navarro took off his hat when he entered. "Mrs. De Aquirre, how lovely to see you again. Thank you for having me in your home."

"We are honored to have you here, Mr. Navarro. Laffit, please get Mr. Navarro some iced tea."

"Oh, I don't need anything. I'm fine. I was hoping that the three of us could just sit and talk for a few moments."

"Certainly." They sat in silence at the wooden family table. Finally, Navarro cleared his throat and spoke.

"Mrs. De Aquirre, I'm sure you know how proud we all are of the wonderful success Laffit has made at the track. He is an outstanding jockey."

"Si, he is very talented."

---

[1] *Stud Book y Estadistica*, Hipódromo Presidente Remón, "Laffit Pincay Jr. Day" Hollywood Park, July 13, 2003.

"Very. So much so that he has caught the attention of Mr. Fred Hooper in Miami."

His mother looked over at Laffit with a scowl. Laffit suppressed the smile trying to twist his mouth upward.

"He would like to fly Laffit to Florida to have him ride for him. Mr. Hooper is the gentleman who brought ..."

But Rosario interrupted him.

"I know who is he."

"If Mr. Hooper likes what he sees, there's a good possibility he'll offer Laffit a contract."

Rosario lowered her gaze.

"I understand you may have concerns, Mrs. De Aquirre, but I will accompany Laffit to Florida where I will personally watch over him. Mr. Hooper would like us to fly out next Sunday after the last race. He wants to put us up in a very nice hotel in Miami."

Rosario said not a word. Navarro was puzzled by the silence.

"Mrs. De Aquirre, this is a rare opportunity that is being presented to your son. Surely you want him to take advantage of it?"

"Mr. Navarro, thank you very much. I will talk this over with my husband." With that, Rosario stood, letting the man know the conversation was over.

Navarro gathered his hat and headed to the door.

Once there he turned to Laffit's mother. "Your son has an enormous career ahead of him, Mrs. De Aquirre. He's going to be famous one day and make you proud, make Panama proud. I am sure you don't want to hold him back."

"Thank you for your visit, Mr. Navarro. I will let you know what my husband has to say."

When his stepfather came home, Laffit overheard his mother in the bedroom relate what had happened.

"He is not even eighteen-years-old. He is too young."

"You cannot stop him, Rosario. This is his dream," her husband gently advised.

"But he is too young to leave his family."

Laffit had been listening quietly from the kitchen during this discussion but finally stepped into the room.

"Mama, I'm going to meet Mr Hooper, whether you say yes or no."

"Not without my permission."

"Mama, I want to do this. I *have* to do this."

Rosario looked at her son. His gaze was set. In the past two years she had watched her son go from a boy with boundless energy to a man with steely determination. It was a man's eyes she was gazing into now. She knew he would not be deterred.

Though the whole notion of her son going so far away terrified Rosario, she also knew it was useless to fight what Navarro was offering. Even she sensed there was something special about her son and his talent.

She simply exhaled. Why fight the inevitable?

Rosario gave her consent to Navarro and it was agreed that they would leave on Sunday evening and return the following Tuesday.

"You will make sure this Mr. Hooper does not take advantage of my son?"

"I promise you, I will look out for Laffit."

"I have heard things about these wealthy horse owners. Some of it's not good. They take advantage. I'm counting on you, Mr. Navarro."

Navarro understood and nodded his agreement.

"You will see, Mrs. De Aquirre. This is a wonderful beginning for Laffit."

Miami dazzled the young man. It was sensory overload the elegant hotel, the lush greenery, the fancy cars, and the beautiful girls. Everything looked scrubbed clean and Technicolor beautiful. But Laffit knew to stay focused. He was there for one thing only, to impress Fred Hooper. Palm trees and gorgeous blondes would have to wait.

They arrived at the track at 8 A.M. on Monday morning. Laffit couldn't believe he was actually at the famous Hialeah Park Racetrack but there before his eyes were the salmon-colored flamingos and the elegant steps leading up to the even more elegant turf club, places he'd only seen in pictures.

Even the stables were impressive. Stalls looked freshly painted, tacking was highly polished, and horses were immaculately groomed. An astonishing number of people could be seen bustling around the stables, hard at work. The intense energy level at Hialeah, compared to the laid back one at home, struck the young jockey immediately and forcefully. This was the big league and he knew it.

After a quick tour of the stables, Laffit was brought to Fred Hooper's crowded office and introduced to a tall, gentle man with a strong handshake.

"You've got a good grip, Laffit. Strong hands. I like that in a jockey." Hooper smiled at him.

Navarro translated and Laffit smiled an embarrassed smile.

"I've heard good things about you, young man. What do you say to riding one of my horses around the track here? Let me see what you can do."

Navarro translated and Laffit muttered, "Okay," a small bit of English he had mastered.

The groom brought the horse and helped Laffit mount, then gently led them out the barn toward the track.

"Just exercise her for a half mile," Hooper shouted to Laffit as he left.

But exercising the horse was not what Laffit had in mind. This was the ride of his life, it would determine everything. He could not just ride, he needed to impress.

With a swift kick, Laffit gave the horse the signal to gallop. He was happy to find her alert and responsive. After a short distance, he decided to open her up. With remarkable speed Laffit propelled the animal forward using his strong arms to thrust the horse's neck out. The wind slapped his face as he kept his head low to the horse's neck, molding his body to her's, aiding the aerodynamics. The fragrant air, the sunshine on his face, the palm trees in his peripheral vision excited him almost as much as the ride he was on. He was riding well and knew it. After they crossed the finish line, he eased the horse down and patted her shoulder, thanking her for the good job she'd done.

He slipped off the saddle and walked the tired horse back into the barn. The smile he saw on Hooper's face told him everything.

"My goodness," said Hooper, "you know you had that little girl going at forty-six and change? The boys down there called to tell me that was the fastest workout of the morning." Hooper was beaming like a proud papa.

Navarro translated and Laffit grinned.

"Good" he knew how to say but tried to remain cool.

"How about we all go into my office and the three of us have a little talk?" Hooper boomed.

When Hooper turned to lead the way, Navarro gave Laffit a thumb's up. His dream of going to America was about to be realized.

The agreement was straightforward. Laffit would be under contract to Hooper for three years. For the duration of the contract he would exercise and ride Hooper's horses for $500 per month. If he won a race he would be entitled to a 10 percent share of the purse. He would only be allowed to ride other trainer's horses when Hooper didn't have a horse in a race. Taxes, living expenses and the 20 percent he would have to pay an agent to book his other rides—when he got an agent—would have to come out of Laffit's earnings.

In Panama, Laffit had been earning roughly $800 to $1,200 a week, sometimes more. Agreeing to Hooper's contract was a huge financial gamble. It meant taking a large pay cut now, hoping that down the line—after the three years, when he had established himself in the U.S.—Laffit would be earning larger sums. It was a gamble on himself he was willing to take.

"I will arrange for the residency papers to be sent to the U.S. Consulate in Panama City and as soon as they are approved, you can come back and we'll get you all set up here."

The men shook hands and Laffit and Navarro went off for a celebratory lunch. Now he could enjoy all the beautiful sights!

Once he was home the excitement he had hoped to share was muted.

"I don't think that contract is fair to you. Three years is too long," one friend challenged.

"But Hooper wouldn't go for just a year."

"Why isn't an agent helping you with this?" another friend wanted to know.

"I'll get an agent when I get my residency papers and am in America."

"You know Baeza had to pay to get out of his contract, it was so unfair. It cost him $100,000!"

"You don't know if that figure is true, Carlos. Look, this is my chance to ride in the States. This is how I have to do it."

His mother said little. Instead, she pursed her lips.

"Why isn't anybody happy for me?" Laffit wailed.

On the first Monday of each month, Laffit traveled to the U.S. Embassy, filled with anticipation, anxious to receive the promised residency papers that would allow him into America. Each month he was told they were not there.

"Maybe it's a good thing," his mother offered, "you have a wonderful life here. Why would you want to leave all this?" Laffit did not answer.

Laffit with family and friends in front of the home in Panama he bought for his mother.

His mother was right. Life in Panama had become exceedingly good. Laffit's sudden celebrity status and his racy white Mustang brought him the admiration of men and the attention of women. He'd also managed to give his mother something she'd always wanted, a home of her own. No longer did the family have to be confined to a three-room apartment, sharing a bathroom with seventeen other people. The house was a dream come true for Rosario.

Still, Laffit's dreams centered on America.

After seven agonizing months of traveling to the consulate and finding no papers, worry began to grind in his stomach. Laffit had to face the sad truth. Hooper was not going to send for him.

More determined than ever to race in the United States, Laffit spotted a golden opportunity when he was given a U.S. work visa to race in Puerto Rico. Without telling anyone, the minute the race was over he would board a plane to New York and head for Aqueduct Racetrack. Once there he would somehow find another American owner to sponsor him.

Laffit had no contacts, had never been to New York, but worst of all, did not speak more than a handful of words in English.

In Puerto Rico, Laffit ran into a man he had known in Panama, Roberto Delaguardia. Delaguardia revealed that by chance, he too was going to Aqueduct as soon as the meet in Puerto Rico was over. Though the man was not a jockey, he was friendly with trainers and agents. And best of all, he spoke English and could translate. Delaguardia, knowing

Laffit's reputation as a rider, agreed to show him around and to introduce him to some of the people he knew.

Once in New York, Delaguardia told Laffit, "I want you to meet a great agent," and introduced him to Camillo Marin at Aqueduct Racetrack. Marin, Laffit remembered immediately, was the agent who handled Braulio Baeza's career.

"You've got a pretty impressive record, Laffit," Marin said. "I think the owner I'm working with might be interested in you."

Laffit crossed his fingers as the man picked up his phone and made a call. He dared not show his excitement.

"Hey, how ya doin?" Marin spoke into the phone. Listen, I've got a young jockey here that I think you might be interested in. He's a Panamanian, and he's won a lot of races." There was a pause as the man on the other end asked a question.

"His name is Laffit Pincay Jr."

Laughter could be heard coming over the phone.

"You do? " Marin said, looking at Laffit with surprise in his eyes.

Marin covered the phone, "How did you get into the U.S.?" Marin asked Laffit. Delaguardia translated.

"I had a race in Puerto Rico. I have a sixty-day visa."

Marin related the information.

"Will do," Marin said into the phone, then hung up.

"Well, my owner is real interested in you. Real interested. But he says you're already under contract."

Laffit felt caught. Delaguardia was surprised at this news too. Laffit hadn't told him about Fred Hooper.

"That was Fred Hooper on the other end of the phone," Marin told them, "the man you're under contract to."

There was a stunned silence from Laffit and Delaguardia.

After a moment, all three men started to laugh.

Laffit spoke rapidly and Delaguardia quickly translated. Laffit told Marin of going to the consulate every month. He explained how he hadn't heard a word from Hooper in seven months and how he assumed he'd changed his mind.

"No, he hasn't changed his mind," Marin explained, "Things sometimes go a bit slow when you're dealing with the government. Believe me, he's interested. Mr. Hooper wants to know much longer you have on your visa?"

"Fifty-four days."

"Well, as long as you're here, he wants to fly you to Chicago and have you race a few horses over at Arlington. What do you say?"

"Great."

One day later, Delaguardia was on his way back home and Laffit and his new agent, Camillo Marin, were on a plane to Chicago. For Laffit's first race at Arlington Park Racetrack, Hooper decided to take the mount from another jockey to put Laffit on Teacher's Art. Hooper gambled that the gutsy Panamanian would make it worth the double jockey fee.

Hooper's instincts were right. On July 1, 1966 in his first race in the United States, Laffit won. The high from this win was even greater than Laffit imagined it would be. He was actually racing—and winning—in the United States and couldn't believe his good fortune. In the next two weeks Laffit won eight out of his first eleven races, including his first U.S. Stakes race, the Hyde Park Stakes on Olympia Site.

"Mama, I just won a $30,000 race!" Laffit yelled into the phone.

"Laffit! Did you have your underpants inside out?"

"Si, mama."

"That's why you won."

Two weeks later Hooper called Laffit and told him to get back to Panama. His papers were waiting for him at the U.S. Consulate.

Preparing for his move was a whirlwind for Laffit. First he had to go to the Mayo Clinic for physicals and inoculations, then there was the visit to the American Consulate to collect his papers. A man with a handlebar mustache presented Laffit with a large, beige envelope.

"Do not open this," he instructed gruffly. "When you get to Immigration at the airport in the United States, hand this to them. Good luck." Then with a small smile he added, "Make us proud."

Laffit kept the envelope tucked in his drawer at home under his shirts. Every night before going to bed, he checked to make sure it was still there. This envelope was his ticket to paradise.

Finally, he handed over the keys to his car to his brother-in-law, and packed the boots and pants his mother bought for him for his first race—his good-luck charms. Plus his underwear, folded inside-out. Naturally.

The closer the departure, the more aware Laffit was of all he was leaving behind and premature pangs of homesickness began. Though there was no doubt that he would go, Laffit was acutely aware that he was truly leaving home and it was a lot to be leaving.

The group at the airport was a depressed lot and though they'd all known for months that this day would come, it felt too soon.

"Mama, I'll be back."

His mother didn't even respond. She just cried into his shoulder and held on to his arm with a firm grip.

No matter how many times he said it, no one believed him.

"I'll be back," he repeated.

In his heart, though, he knew that if things went as he hoped, he'd only be back for visits. He desperately wanted to succeed in America. He had seen the good life in Miami and Chicago. He was eager to live it.

Leaving Panama in 1966. Note the beige envelope in his hand.

As the plane taxied, Laffit watched out the window as everyone he loved diminished in size. They waved frantically, some of the young boys jumping in the air, until his plane lifted from the ground and then they were gone from sight. He felt such mixed emotions, he was finally going to America but he was leaving behind the people who meant the most to him. Then he fingered the beige envelope. This was his future. And all doubts disappeared.

USA

CHAPTER 3

Fred Hooper's trainer, Cotton Tinsley, and Camillo Marin were at the airport to greet Laffit when his plane landed in Chicago. Laffit had met Tinsley at Aqueduct and was happy to see a familiar face. Marin waved to Laffit as he made his way through the line at Immigration.

Once he reached the head of the line, the uniformed man behind the desk unsealed the precious envelope, flipped through the stack of papers, and looked up.

"Welcome to the United States, Mr. Pincay."

The man stamped his passport and Laffit was finally, officially, in the States.

Outside, Marin led him to a fancy black Town Car. "This is some car," he told his agent.

"Marge Everett is a good friend of Mr. Hooper's and she sent it," Marin said. "She wanted to welcome you to Chicago."

Laffit stepped in and adjusted to the darkness. He reached over and touched decanters and wine glasses neatly arranged inside the sleek interior.

"Are you thirsty, Laffit?" Marin inquired.

"A little."

"What would you like, Coke, Sprite, or champagne?" his agent asked.

"Do they have anything diet?"

"This is America, Laffit, you can have anything you want," Marin replied.

I sure hope so, Laffit thought to himself.

The apartments at the Arlington Park Racetrack are situated behind the track, where it was not unusual for a jockey and his agent to bunk together. Not only does it save money, it is often a necessity. When a jockey is starting out, and especially when he doesn't know the language, he relies on his agent. As agents only have one client, and the two have to travel from racetrack to racetrack during the course of the year, the setup is practical.

The apartment Everett arranged for Laffit and Marin had two bedrooms, a functional kitchen and a large living room with a colored T.V. The proximity to work, needless to say, was extremely handy.

Each morning at 6:30 A.M. Laffit went to the track to work Hooper's horses, usually for two to four hours. Laffit was finally where he dreamed of being and for the most part the experience was even better than he expected.

The only uncomfortable difference Laffit discovered was the refined way in which American jockeys behaved during a race. Though these jockeys were highly competitive, they were not as ruthless as those he rode with in Panama. In Panama, you rode to win and did whatever you needed to do to cross that finish line. If you didn't win, those in attendance felt free to boo and toss garbage at you when you rode your horse off the track. This proved a good incentive to do whatever was needed in order to win.

The jockeys at Arlington immediately set the newcomer straight.

"What did you think you were doing out there, buddy?"

"What are you talking about?"

"You bumped my horse."

"So what?"

"So what? So what? You're not in Panama anymore, that's what. You learn to race properly or you're going to get days."

"Days?"

"Suspended."

And he was. Often. Laffit learned early that if a rider couldn't ride, he couldn't win. When he couldn't win, he couldn't earn. Since Laffit liked winning, the newcomer refined his ways very quickly.

Laffit in Hooper silks with Camillo Marin.

Camillo Marin was a dapper Cuban who knew his way around the track. He'd successfully managed the careers of several Panamanian jockeys—which meant he was skilled at turning a novice into a superstar—exactly what Laffit was hoping for.

But Laffit was used to being independent. Needing Marin to manage his career, and also to negotiate his way in a new country, was uncomfortable for him. He immediately focused on learning the language. Television helped, as did the other Spanish-speaking jockeys who bantered with Laffit and taught him important phrases and customs.

The Spanish jockeys also taught Laffit how to avoid suspensions.

"Laffit, you can't ride so hard here. You have to control yourself."

"And that temper of yours, you've got to watch that. These Americans don't like that."

"I can't help it. I want to win. I get carried away."

"We know, we know. But it can get you into trouble. You have to learn to control yourself. Watch The Shoe when he comes here next week. He's incredible. Nothing bothers him. He's the fiercest competitor out there but when he gets back to the jocks' room, he's as sweet as can be. You'll see. Just watch him."

At the mention of Bill Shoemaker, Laffit was all ears. Shoemaker was his idol, the rider he admired most. Laffit couldn't believe Bill Shoemaker was actually coming to Arlington Park and that he was set to compete against him in two separate races.

"Mama, guess who I'm riding against next week?"
"Laffit!! She yelled, "Juan, it's Laffit on the phone! Who, who are you riding against?"
"Bill Shoemaker!"
"No!" His mother exclaimed. "He is the best, Laffit."
"I know, Mama. But I'm gonna beat him."

The following week Laffit arrived early to the jockeys' room. When Shoemaker walked in, Laffit was startled. His hero was so small. *How can he be so great and make those horses run?* He wondered.

That day, though Shoemaker's horse was favored, to his utter amazement, Laffit beat him to the finish line. That afternoon Laffit rode Teacher's Art for the second time and triumphed over The Shoe.

Laffit could hardly sustain the excitement within his chest. *I just beat the greatest jockey of all time, Bill Shoemaker.*

After the race, Shoemaker came up to him and introduced himself. "You did great out there, kid. I've heard a lot about you and people were right, you're gonna be terrific. Hell, you already are. Are you going to Marge Everett's tonight? Maybe I can make some money back from you playing poker."

Marge Everett, the owner of Arlington Park Racetrack, was an easygoing, gracious hostess who enjoyed giving lavish parties for her many friends. Her sumptuous house, annexed to the racetrack, made it a convenient place to socialize. In those days there was no racing on Sundays so Saturday night was the perfect time to gather for some fun and frolic after a long week of competitive racing. Laffit was happy to be invited.

Marge's uniformed staff floated around the house offering platters of hor d'oeuvres and a variety of drinks. A man in a white jacket sat at the piano providing just the right kind of music. That is, when Merv Griffin (or some other celebrity) wasn't playing. Jockeys, trainers, and owners—plus celebrities Ron and Nancy Reagan, Johnny Mathis and Jimmy Durante among others—could occasionally be spotted at the bar or playing cards.[2]

The stakes at the poker tables—hot beds of action—were high. Laffit shied away from the games not just for financial reasons but because he didn't know how to play and didn't know how to keep up with the banter. He often stayed at the bar chatting with fellow Panamanian jockeys.

That evening Laffit met Desi Arnaz at the bar. Laffit tried not to show his excitement, sharing a Scotch with one of the most famous men in Hollywood, but he was mesmerized by the Cuban bandleader and was delighted to converse with him in Spanish. Desi complimented Laffit's expert rid-

[2] CNN, Larry King Live, April 6, 2001.

ing that afternoon, beating out Shoemaker. As the conversation progressed, Laffit confessed his ambitions to the entertainer. "I don't just want to win," he told Desi, "I want to be the leading jockey!"

"Take things easy," Desi chuckled, "Don't be so ambitious. Don't rush. Just remember, with patience and saliva, the elephant can screw the ant." They both laughed heartily.

When Laffit got back to the apartment, he called his mother.

"Mama, I met Desi Arnaz."

"What a handsome man," his mother commented.

"And I met Bill Shoemaker."

"You did? What was he like?"

"He is a very humble man."

"He is?"

"He had to be. I beat him today."

His mother shrieked on the other end of the phone.

Shoemaker, it turned out, was as unpretentious and open as people said. And he didn't get sore over a loss. In the jocks' room one day after a race, Laffit was frustrated. He'd tried everything to win the race but came in a disappointing second. Shoemaker came up from behind and patted him on the back and whispered before he moved on, "Don't lose your mind out there, kid, cause when you lose your mind, you lose your ass."

Laffit took note of the advice.

Though his first season was not a full one, Laffit nonetheless rode ninety-two winners and won $612,918. Few jockeys' had ever had so sensational a beginning. He was *the* hot commodity in racing.

Marge Everett was especially generous with her time and support of Laffit. She believed he was a special talent, and realized how hard the transition was for the newcomer. She went out of her way to make him comfortable.

At Marge's elegant, though raucous, dinner parties, Laffit began to enjoy the social aspect of racing—even though he couldn't eat or drink much that was offered.

These parties helped Laffit deal with the extreme loneliness he was experiencing. Though anxious to get to America, once he was without the support of his family and friends from back home, Laffit felt isolated. Creating further tension, Camillo Marin began borrowing large sums of money from Laffit.

Laffit had been warned early on by fellow jockeys that he had to be scrupulous in his dealings with the Internal Revenue Service. Every penny earned had to be accounted for. Being in the U.S. with residential status meant he had to obey the laws of the country rigorously. There could be no possibility of his actions, financial or otherwise, being misinterpreted.

Laffit wanted to pay Marin his agent fees each week by check, as he had been instructed to do, but Marin insisted on cash. It didn't take long for Laffit to realize that Marin was using a loophole to avoid paying taxes.

The two fought and tensions began to intrude on the otherwise successful relationship. Compounding the problem was that after a few months Laffit began to master a good deal of the language. He wasn't as easily manipulated anymore.

The season at Arlington Park ended and Marin and Pincay moved to Hawthorne Racetrack in Cicero, Illinois. From there they headed to New York and Aqueduct Racetrack. The season there turned out to be remarkable with Laffit winding up second in the standings, something unheard of for a newcomer.

Perhaps best of all for Laffit was the fact that many of the jockeys at Aqueduct were Spanish. In New York, however, Laffit felt confined living in the Marin household with Camillo's wife and children. Luckily his jockey friends, including Angel Cordero, Eddie Belmonte and Manuel Ycaza often took Laffit dancing in Manhattan. Laffit was delighted to enjoy some female companionship again—and men with whom he could freely converse.

One afternoon when Laffit finished riding early, he went into the grandstand at Aqueduct where Camillo Marin often conducted business. On this particular day Marin was talking with Bill Radkovich, a California-based contractor who, among other things, built the Hollywood Park turf course. Laffit arrived just as Radkovich was leaving. Marin turned to Laffit and asked, "Do you know who that man is?"

"Isn't he an owner?"

"Yes he is. He owns Wilbur Clark."

"I thought so. He's a really nice man. Who were those pretty young women he was with?" Laffit wanted to know.

"Those are his daughters, Millie and Linda."

"They are beautiful. Especially the one with the big brown eyes. I remember seeing her at the paddock once. What a smile she has."

Laffit would have no way of knowing then how the girl with the big brown eyes would change his life.

After successful runs at Arlington Park, Hawthorne Racetrack and then Aqueduct, Marin and Laffit traveled to Santa Anita Park for Laffit's first season in the California sun. At first glance, he fell in love with the racetrack

Santa Anita Racetrack is located in Arcadia, California. It is lush with flowers and greenery and has the majestic San Gabriel Mountains behind it creating a magnificent backdrop against which the races are run. Palm trees and snow capped mountains frame the track making it truly one of the most spectacular locales for all of racing.

Could there be a more glorious place to be, Laffit wondered, than here? To add to the attractiveness of the surroundings, Hollywood turned out to be a mere half hour ride away. Stars often dropped by to wish the young, handsome new rider luck, or thank him for a great ride, or to invite him for a drink or dinner, or to a party after the races.

Undoubtedly for Laffit, the greatest attribute of all to recommend Santa Anita was the weather. For someone who had practically frozen in Illinois and New York over the past few months, the warm weather thawed his soul. With a mere two percent body fat, cold penetrated Laffit deeply—especially when he was at the track in the early morning exercising horses. Some days he felt as though he never could warm up. California sunshine beat snow any day.

Living arrangements were also better there. Laffit had his own room at the Westerner Hotel, which gave him a greater sense of independence. With his English improving, he also felt more confident about taking a more active role in his business. His riding was, as always, remarkable—but controlling his weight, always something he was vigilant about, was starting to become a challenge. He became stricter with himself about what he consumed.

Even though Laffit was racing well, Hooper didn't necessarily own the best horses. It was frustrating for Laffit to watch other jockeys win on horses he was sometimes asked to ride but couldn't and it was downright painful when they collected what could have been his earnings.

Laffit and Marin arrived at Santa Anita just as the meet was about to begin. A few days later, on Laffit's twentieth birthday, December 29, he decided to treat himself to a nice meal at the Westerner and Marin accompanied him. He had had a great day on the track, beating out Walter Blum, a jockey who was considered one of the best at the time. The win felt like a great omen for his birthday and the coming year.

Laffit and Marin went to the bar while they waited for a table and there met Millie Radkovich, the daughter of Bill Radkovich. Millie's date that night was comedian Guy Marks. Laffit remembered her. Millie was open and friendly and began talking to Laffit, which did not please Marks. When Millie found out it was Laffit's birthday, she insisted he and Camillo sit with them for dinner.

Laffit's English by this point, though not fluent, was enough for him to be able to communicate. Some words still eluded him, however. When the waitress asked what he wanted to eat, he couldn't make himself understood. Finally Laffit pointed to his ribs. Millie was the one to solve the mime. "I think he wants spare ribs for dinner." The table broke out in laughter, causing all eyes in the restaurant to turn to them. Including a set of beautiful brown eyes on the other side of the room.

With a twinkle, Millie said, "I want you to meet my sister, Linda, she's here tonight," she told Laffit and went to fetch her. Linda was having dinner with a group of people, including Walter Blum, the jockey Laffit had beaten twice that day.

Linda and Laffit had immediate chemistry. A flirtatious air permeated the table and when Linda—reluctantly—said she really ought to get back to the other table, Laffit offered to accompany her. It became a night of musical chairs. Linda and Laffit spent the evening with eyes locked on one another. When Laffit said he would like to see her home, Blum acquiesced.

As the two men stood to leave, a frustrated Blum whispered to Laffit,

"You beat me on the track today and now you beat me with the girl."

Laffit could only shrug. What could he say? He was smitten.

That night, Laffit kissed Linda goodnight. It was the perfect birthday gift.

From then on, Laffit and Linda were inseparable. His longing for Panama began to diminish.

EARLY DAYS

CHAPTER 4

inda Radkovich and Laffit Pincay were married on December 16, 1967, at St. Victor's Parish Church in West Hollywood. Bridesmaids, carrying out the winter Christmas theme, wore crimson dresses with white fur hats and car-

Wedding party: Linda's father Bill Radkovich, Linda, Laffit, Laffit's mother Rosario and his sister Margie. December 16, 1967

ried fur muffs. Millie, Linda's sister and matchmaker, was the maid of honor. Newspapers hailed it a royal racing wedding, the blending of two prominent names in horse racing, Radkovich and Pincay. The bride's father was delighted with the union.

Bride and groom.

The reception in the ballroom at the Beverly Hilton Hotel was lavish and though the bride and groom were barely twenty-one, pictures from that day make it evident that this was a love match destined to last.

Linda, as it turned out, was more than simply a devoted wife, she was a woman with seemingly limitless knowledge when it came to horses and racing. It wasn't merely that she'd grown up with a father who owned horses; Linda was an expert in her own right. She was comfortable with trainers and owners and liked to trade complex statistics with them (which horse won which Belmont Stakes, which trainer preferred what jockey, who used a left whip, what the payoff was for the second place horse for any particular Kentucky Derby.) And she shared all this knowledge in her own unassuming way.

Linda also had a keen appreciation for her husband's special talent. She knew he was more than just a good jockey, she believed him to be the best there was and so she dedicated herself to creating a world in which Laffit could devote himself fully to his riding.

Despite her quiet ways, however, Linda did not suffer fools gladly. If Linda was at the clubhouse having lunch and discovered that someone at her table had bet on a jockey other than her husband in any given race, she would banish that person from the table.

Her protectiveness was intense. Once when Laffit rode one of her father's horses and it threw Laffit off, she was furious with her dad for having put her husband in harm's way. Everyone—including her family—knew Linda was Laffit's greatest champion.

The season at Santa Anita started just a few days after their wedding. The couple moved into an apartment on Duarte Road in Arcadia and instead of a honeymoon, which there was no time to take, they splurged on furniture for their first home together. Linda turned out to be the perfect housewife. Though she grew up in a wealthy home where she had been catered to by servants and chefs, Linda was a wonderful cook and homemaker.

The racetrack was less than five minutes from their apartment and Linda often accompanied her husband to watch him race, especially on weekends when there was an air of excitement at the track. Massive crowds filled the stands cheering their favorites along.

Linda's designated table at the turf club was usually filled with her sister Millie, Linda's friend from grammar school Roseann, and Naila Winfield, who was the wife of a trainer, plus a constantly changing cast of celebrities, jockeys' wives, and friends.

While Millie and Roseann were naturally outgoing, Linda had a softer personality. People often commented that there was a vulnerable quality about Linda which caused people, including her sister, to act protectively toward her. That quality was also a magnet for men and sometimes drove Laffit crazy. Despite—or because of—the powerful love the two shared, there were moments of jealousy when Laffit feared Linda was flirting, or being flirted with, or vice versa.

After the races, the group, now including Laffit, would gravitate to local restaurants that racing fans frequented: Talk of the Town, The Derby or Domenico's were all welcoming establishments with good bars, lively music and great food (though Laffit could hardly attest to the quality of the food, only sampling it as he did.)

The chosen haunt of the evening would be enlivened when jockeys and their entourages burst through the front doors. Laffit's infectious laugh was often the first things patrons heard when they entered. It was a magical time in Laffit's life.

The first full year riding in the United States, Laffit had finished sixth in money ($1,933,618) and twelfth in racing wins. The following year, 1968, Laffit and Linda enjoyed even more successes with Laffit ending up third in the money rankings ($2,303,837) and fifth in wins (266). It was an amazing—and fast— ride to the top.[3] On April 27, 1968, Laffit tied Bill Shoemaker's single-day Hollywood Park record. Laffit had won six races out of nine mounts. And Laffit accomplished this feat, on of all days, "Bill Shoemaker Day."

The following year's numbers were not up to Laffit's standards, in part due to suspensions and also because of an accident he had while racing at Hollywood Park. Not being able to ride because of injury frustrated Laffit. Not being able to ride because of suspensions was another matter entirely.

Luckily, suspensions in riding usually do not take effect immediately. Prior commitments can generally be honored and a jockey can ride for the next day or two until stewards determine if a suspension will take effect, when it will occur, and how long it will be for. Though some stewards' rulings

---

[3] Hollywood Park, "Laffit Pincay Jr. Day," July 13, 2003.

felt downright unfair to Laffit (and were occasionally argued,) for the most part the nature of the business meant
you accepted them without complaint. Luckily one of the
suspensions Laffit got that year did not prevent his riding in
the Alcibiades Stakes race where he won the $50,000 purse.

At long last, his contract with Fred Hooper came to an
end. Hooper wanted to extend it but Laffit politely declined.
Though he was grateful to Fred Hooper for the opportunity
Hooper had given him, one of the important things Laffit
had learned during the past three years was that the major
races (the money races where earnings were higher) took
place in New York and California. Having set his sights on
being the country's leading rider in money, Laffit knew that
to achieve that he had to concentrate on riding in those two
states. Going with Hooper to Chicago deeply affected his
earning capacity, something he did not want to jeopardize
any longer.

Happily he was riding great horses now, something that
had frustrated him when he was under contract and couldn't.
Hooper, for his part, was generous in acquiescing. Laffit had
done well for Hooper and he knew Laffit couldn't be held
back any longer. It was time for Laffit to move on.

Laffit knew that even riding the best horses didn't mean
that things would necessarily go smoothly. And they didn't.
Laffit would have earned more the year he left Hooper but
for an ankle break and Laffit's unique bent for self-diagnosis.

Two weeks after he'd been put into a cast, he decided he was healed and removed the cast himself—with a hammer.

"Are you crazy?" Linda asked when she came into the living room and saw the crumbled plaster on the floor.

"I heal fast. I don't need this anymore." Laffit said as he chipped away.

"Not in two weeks. The doctor said you need to be in a cast for six to eight weeks."

"Don't worry. I'm sure I'm all healed."

Linda knew the real reason Laffit wanted the cast off. He had his sights set on being leading rider.

With the cast in pieces in front of him, Laffit stood and attempted to walk across the room. He didn't make it two steps before he fell.

"I told you," Linda said, "But you wouldn't listen. Oh, no, you knew better than the doctor."

Laffit lay on the floor clutching his throbbing ankle.

"You have to call the doctor," Laffit moaned.

"Why do you do these things to yourself? *You* call the doctor."

"I can't get to the phone. Please, Linda, it hurts."

"When are you going to learn?" Linda had experienced Laffit's self-doctoring before and been frustrated by it.

"Please call him."

"Why, so you can do this again next week?"

Laffit was now writhing in pain. He hadn't realized that the cast had kept his ankle immobile and therefore pain-free.

"Hurts, doesn't it? Pretty hard to ride a horse like that." Linda sat in a side chair with her arms folded in front of her.

"Linda, please, I beg you to call. You know those pearl earrings you wanted? I'll get them for you, I promise."

"I don't want jewelry, Laffit. I want a sensible husband who takes care of himself."

As usual, however, Linda relented. She called the doctor and told him what had happened. Even across the room Laffit could hear the doctor yelling through the phone, "You tell that little son of a gun to get in my office right away!"

When she hung up, Linda turned to him,

"And I will take those earrings. They'll be a good reminder to you to do what the doctor tells you from now on."

But all their disagreements were not as playfully resolved. Though very much in love, and successful beyond their wildest imaginations, there were dark undercurrents that flowed beneath their marriage, undercurrents that threatened to obliterate everything they held dear.

Just two years married, the undertow yanked and brought them both under.

THE DOWNHILL RACE

CHAPTER 5

I
t was just another fight but in reality it was the start of an ugly downward spiral that neither of them could predict, or even prevent. It began on New Year's Eve, 1969. Linda and Laffit were invited to Dr. Ruben Marchosky's house in Arcadia, California, to celebrate the holiday. Dr. Marchosky was their family internist who, over the years, had become a friend and with whom they often socialized. Though Linda had initially agreed to the plans, that day she changed her mind. She wanted to be with her friends, she told Laffit, none of who were going to be at this party. Laffit reminded her that they had accepted the invitation a

month ago, it was too late to back out. Besides, he was look-ing forward to the party. She would have to make the best of it.

Their fights of late were always the same—she wanted to be with her friends; he wanted to be with his. While he liked most of her friends, he didn't want to spend all their time with them. Conversely, Linda knew Laffit's friends and didn't like any of them. His friends were the ones he was running around with at night while she was at home. They were the party boys who invited girls to join them for dinner, girls who enjoyed flirting with her husband. His friends spelled trouble.

Being a famous jockey meant meeting women free with their affections, and admiration—especially with charming, good-looking jockeys who knew how to have a good time. Laffit had a roving eye, he admitted it. He was not proud of his dalliances, but he forgave himself. He was, after all, Latin and Latin men are another breed. It was a special culture into which he was born. Didn't his own father do the same thing? Didn't his friends? Laffit simply did not subscribe to the American set of gender role models that Linda grew up with. He had his own standards.

But there was more to his self-forgiveness. From the be-ginning, Laffit had put himself on a punishing regimen in order to achieve the kind of success he wanted. He exercised beyond reason, he controlled every morsel of food that passed his lips, and rode horses with more intensity than anyone had ever seen. And he had done all this for almost a decade.

He allowed himself these occasional dalliances not because he believed them right but because he simply couldn't control all aspects of his life at all times and this was the one area in which he felt he could compromise. It was the unspoken tradeoff he made with himself. It was not that he didn't love his wife. He did. He certainly didn't wish to hurt her. But he did, and for whatever reason, he couldn't stop.

What Laffit demanded of himself each day in order to win took extreme, some say superhuman, discipline. There were no days off because of birthdays, or Christmas or an anniversary. He exercised every day of the year. He was at the track by nine thirty each day before a race, jogging or walking. He often rode eight races a day, exerting a kind of Herculean energy needed to dominate horses in race after race, without the fuel of food to help him. In addition, he took water pills, diet pills, starved himself, and still he rode to victory.

For many years he told everyone he limited himself to 850 calories a day. He was too ashamed to tell them the truth. In reality, he was consuming much, much less. His daily diet consisted of:

BREAKFAST

Coffee (lots of it throughout the day)

1 piece of toast (every other day)

LUNCH

Nothing

DINNER

1 ounce of rice

2 ounces of chicken or steak

If Laffit felt particularly weak, he might add an egg in the morning (perhaps once a week.) On occasion, he would add a vegetable to his dinner. Sometimes he had a little salad (lettuce, with tomato, cucumber or mushroom) with lemon and vinegar or fresh spinach with lemon and vinegar. If Laffit thought his weight was under control, he would increase the chicken or beef to three ounces. For a man five feet, one-inch tall and 117 pounds whose goal weight was always *less*, the challenge was formidable.

In reality, for decades, he consumed no more than 350 calories on any given day.

The United Nations declares starvation rations as 800 calories per day. [4] Laffit not only ate too little, he exerted energy, which depleted his body further. That he did not collapse on a daily basis was baffling to fellow jockeys, trainers and doctors. How did his body go on? What, beyond sheer will, could allow him to continue?

Celebratory dinners after big wins, where everyone wanted to meet the winning jockey, meant exercising even more self-control. While other diners around him feasted on steak and baked potatoes, washed down with Dom Perignon, Laffit carved out three ounces of chicken on the plate before him. Because he was celebrating he added the

---

[4] "Millions Face Starvation Rations as Aid Dries Up" by Hamish McDonald, *THE AGE*, February 10, 2004.

extra ounce of meat and sometimes, *sometimes*, a glass of wine into which he poured a packet of Sweet N'Low. (Laffit claimed this greatly improved the taste. Wealthy owners pouring $400 bottles of Puligny Montrachet were appalled.) Potatoes were ignored, vegetables and salads refused. Deserts were easier to dismiss because he could tell waiters before-hand not to place them before him. What was harder to ig-nore was a tempting piece of broccoli that sat beside his small piece of meat. If he did have that glass of wine, he knew he would pay for it the next day with hours in the sweatbox.

Laffit, unfortunately, was not built to be a jockey. From the beginning he'd been told his frame was too large. To compete, he would have to make himself unnaturally smaller by controlling his size, which meant watching his weight, at all times, something he began to do as a teenager. Other jockeys, like Bill Shoemaker, were by nature small-boned. It was easier for them to maintain the necessary weight. Angel Cordero could also eat normally and only rarely had to go into the sweatbox to lose a pound before a race. Laffit and the sweatbox, unfortunately, were well acquainted.

On the rare occasion when he "indulged" (had a drink with friends, or had a salad), Laffit would pull off the weight by going into the dreaded sweatbox for hours. Anytime be-tween eight thirty in the morning and one in the afternoon, when the races started, Laffit would sometimes sweat off as much as six pounds of water. Though many doctors warned him about the tremendous strain this practice put on his body, he knew he would continue with it. He had to. He had to lose weight for the weigh-in before each race. If he were too heavy, a trainer might take him off an upcoming race that had been agreed upon. Laffit didn't want to lose the mount. He *had* to race. He had to *win*.

It wasn't just the struggle to keep his weight down, it was also the constant exercising he forced upon himself. Mornings he wasn't in the sweatbox, Laffit ran miles around the track, often he trotted horses, then came home to walk more miles on the treadmill. It was a grueling routine he forced upon himself every single day. If he let up for even a day, he knew he would pay for it. So he didn't.

Because of his constant struggle with weight, Laffit was forced into a pattern of dieting and reducing. It would be years before he met a nutritionist who taught him how to balance proteins and carbohydrates and refined his eating habits.

Laffit often triumphed on the track, but the constant strain on his body was also a drain on his psyche. Sometimes, he *had* to go out with the guys, to blow off a little steam. He deserved it, didn't he? When you give up so much, when you work so hard, it doesn't feel unreasonable to want to party a little. But wives, he soon realized, don't see it that way.

Laffit grew irritable and so did Linda. He was short-tempered, she was angry, and so the fights began. Whether it was his restrictive diet, or the various pills he was taking, or the constant pressure to win, or whether it was simply his Latin nature, he couldn't be sure.

But the fights seemed always to be about the same things. He wanted to go out with his friends, she wanted to be with hers. Blending the two groups never seemed to work.

A distance grew between them that made them both unhappy. That New Year's Eve Laffit told Linda that he hoped the start of a new year would be good for both of them.

It was a dinner party preceded by cocktails and hors d'oeuvres. Laffit was in a suit and Linda was wearing a beautiful pink dress with a black sash, sporting the sparkly diamond earrings he had given her for Christmas.

"You look really lovely," he told his wife, and meant it.

"Thanks," she replied but didn't seem to take in the compliment.

The Pincays arrived around 9:00 PM and began mingling. The house was bustling with activity. Some of the doctor's Spanish friends recognized Laffit and began conversing with him in their native language.

"Well, Laffit, I owe you a big thanks," said one of the guests.

"What for?"

"I made more money at the track this year betting on you than I did from my practice." Everyone in the small group laughed.

Linda stood behind her husband for a few minutes, listening to the joviality, once again shut out of the conversation. It was something she always resented. Out of the corner of his eye, Laffit could see her growing irritation. She left after a few minutes and went to the bar. Laffit soon followed.

"Why did you leave me?" he said.

"What am I doing here?"

"What are you talking about? These are our friends."

"They aren't my friends, they're yours. You're with your friends. You don't need me."

"Linda, don't start with that again."

"You know I didn't want to be here."

"You agreed to come."

"Well, I wish I hadn't. I want to go home."

"We can't go home. It's ten o'clock. We have to be here until after midnight at least."

"Tell them I'm not feeling well."

"We can't leave this party. It's rude."

"Just take me home and then you can come back to your buddies."

Laffit was fuming but had little choice. Linda was clearly not going to be persuaded to enjoy herself. Laffit found the doctor in his den surrounded by a group of laughing men and women. He whispered in the doctor's ear that Linda had the stomach flu and he was going to take her home. He'd be right back.

"Yes, please come back."

Once in the car, the tension was unleashed.

"It's embarrassing leaving like this," he said.

"I won't be missed, believe me."

"I told the doctor I'd be back after I drop you off."

"Then go back. I don't care. I couldn't stand being there another minute."

The fighting escalated, growing more vicious, each of them hurling names at the other, even striking one another at one point. When he dropped her off at home, he was fuming. He returned to the party hoping to be distracted by the activity and the people. Someone he didn't know grabbed his arm.

"There you are. I've been looking for you! Laffit, settle a bet, will you? Was it Donald Pierce who you beat in the last race on Saturday? I told Jerry here that it was but he doesn't believe me. I've got one hundred dollars riding on this."

"You're right. It was Donald. He was pretty mad at me, too."

Laffit joined the conversation but was distracted. He kept replaying what he'd said to Linda, what she'd said to him, and how they'd hurt each another.

"See Jerry, I told you."

He laughed and smiled with the men but it was no use. He had to go home and apologize. He went to find Marchosky.

"Doctor, I am so sorry, but I'm worried about Linda. She has a fever and I don't want to leave her alone," he lied. "I think I should go back and be with her."

"Of course, Laffit, don't give it a second thought. You'll be missed but please tell Linda we wish her a happy New Year."

"I will. Happy New Year to you, too."

By the time he reached home, true remorse had set in. Why were they so cruel to one another? Why did he feel the need to "escape" home when he knew it caused her so much pain? He knew he loved her and would never leave her. He would have to apologize. It was a new year and they could start over. They loved one another, after all.

The apartment was dark when he let himself in. He stumbled his way into the bedroom and put on the small bathroom light so as not to disturb his wife. He was in the bathroom when he glanced over at the bed and saw Linda wasn't there. He looked down and saw her sprawled on the floor dressed in a pale blue negligee. Her hair was disheveled and her mouth was agape. Something registered in his brain. A panic washed over him.

He ran to her. "Linda!" he yelled but she didn't respond. He reached and turned on the light on the bedside table. The color was drained from her face. On the side table he saw the pill bottle. Her new prescription of Valium was turned on its side, the cap lying beside it, completely empty. He shook Linda but failed to get a response. Her head bobbed back and forth. She didn't even moan. He picked up the phone and called the first place he could think of for help—Dr. Marchosky who lived a few minutes away. Thankfully, Marchosky rushed over immediately.

Neighbors were awakened by the sirens and the rush of the paramedics up the stairs and into their apartment. Burly young men carrying various types of equipment lumbered through their apartment and took over. Laffit stood in the doorway of their bedroom, watching helplessly as strange men hovered over his wife. They barked instructions to one another and into walkie-talkies but it was all a blur to him. He only remembered one of them saying something about a hospital.

"Will my wife be okay?" he asked. Though Dr. Marchosky had told him she would recover, he needed further reassurance.

"We're going to take her to the hospital," the paramedics told him. "Why don't you follow us in your car?"

He saw the neighbors, some in robes, others holding wine glasses, watching as he left his apartment. He realized that their New Year's Eve revelry was muted by the sobering appearance of his wife being carried out on a stretcher. He thanked Dr. Marchosky and rushed to follow the ambulance.

They took Linda to the Emergency Room at Methodist Hospital in Arcadia. Laffit sat alone in the waiting room for hours worrying. His emotions shifted from self-castigation to fear. *Why did I say those things tonight? Why?* He hated himself for having made her so unhappy and he feared what would happen if doctors were unable to save her.

Depression ran in Linda's family but Laffit never imagined it would manifest itself this way. *Please God, let her be okay.*

Worst of all, Laffit knew he had contributed to her un-happiness. *It's all my fault. I know it. This wouldn't have happened if I was a better husband.*

After a few hours the doctor came out and found Laffit.

"Your wife is going to be all right." Laffit crumpled with relief and the doctor caught him.

"Thank you, doctor. Thank you." By now, a floodgate of tears was released. He was so grateful.

"Her vital signs look good. We managed to pump her stomach and get out a lot of the pills before they could do too much damage but I want to observe her overnight. If she stabilizes by the morning, I'll want to move her to the psychiatric unit of the hospital for a few days."

"The psychiatric unit?"

"A suicide attempt is a cry for help. We need to find out why your wife did this."

"Certainly. Whatever you think is best."

"We'll see how she's doing when she's fully conscious. You're a very lucky man, Mr. Pincay."

"Can I see my wife?"

"She's sleeping right now. Why don't you go home and get some rest yourself and come back later in the morning?"

"Whatever you say."

The sky was turning pink when Laffit drove home and the streets were empty. It felt like years since they'd left the apartment last night, less than twelve hours ago, to go to a party. A few people were returning from their New Year's

Eve celebrations. What different evenings they had had, he thought. They were drunk. He was stone cold sober.

The apartment looked frightening when Laffit entered it. Furniture had been pushed aside by paramedics and discarded medical paraphernalia was scattered all over the carpet, especially in the bedroom. He quickly put the room back in order and felt better when it looked normal again. But the image of Linda's body on the floor kept flashing in his mind, even when he closed his eyes.

Beneath all the exhaustion, however, was relief. Linda would be okay, he kept telling himself. Before long she would be back home and they would work out their problems. He was committed to that. They could overcome this, he was sure. Exhausted, he finally drifted off to sleep.

Laffit arrived at the hospital later that morning and found Linda sitting alone in a sunny corner of a large room dressed in a green hospital gown. She was, as the doctor had warned, in the psychiatric unit. Her makeup from the night before was smudged and her hair, normally so smooth and shiny, was tangled. She saw Laffit approach and lowered her eyes.

He kissed her cheek.

"How are you feeling?"

"Better. I want to go home."

"I'm glad you're feeling better."

"I want to go home."

"I know. Look, the doctor said he thought it would be a good idea for you to be here for a few days."

"A few days! I can't stay here. You've got to get me out of here, Laffit. Please. Just take me home. I'm fine."

"I think they can help you."

"I'll do much better at home, I promise you. I'm okay."

Her eyes pleaded with him.

"I'll talk to the doctor."

She reached out for his hand.

"Thank you."

The doctor did not like the idea of Linda leaving.

"I think in light of what's happened, your wife could use some help, don't you agree?"

"I'll make sure she gets some, doctor. I promise. My wife just wants to go home now. I can take care of her myself. I think she'll get better faster at home."

The doctor was not pleased but he released Linda that afternoon. Laffit brought her home and she went straight to their bedroom saying she was tired and wanted to lie down. Laffit followed her into their room.

"Are you hungry? Would you like some food? I'll get you something."

"I'm not hungry." Linda was turning down the bed.

"Your body needs some food to help you recover."

"I'm fine."

"You've just been through an ordeal."

Linda stopped cold and looked directly at Laffit, "I don't want to talk about it, okay?"

He froze. He didn't want to upset her. He promised himself he wouldn't do that anymore.

"Okay," he said.

And they never did talk about it, not ever again.

NEW LIFE

CHAPTER 6

Though deeply shaken by what had happened, Laffit trusted Linda's assurances that she was "fine" and that nothing further needed to be done. They both moved forward, anxious to put the incident behind them. Life resumed its normal rhythms.

During that year, Linda stopped taking birth control pills. Laffit hoped having a child would be good for her. But though they both very much wanted a baby, nothing happened. The pressures of riding may have had something to do with the problem. Jockeys (and their wives) were aware that extreme dieting, over-exercising, and hours spent in the sweatbox often affected sperm count. Nonetheless, they were disappointed. They were ready for a family.

When it came to the end of the racing season in New York, Laffit and Linda decided to make a vacation out of their return. They leased a Cadillac and chose to take the scenic route back to California, a drive they enjoyed tremendously. When they reached Oklahoma, however, and were unpacking, Linda made a heart-wrenching discovery. Her carrying case with her makeup and all of her jewelry had been left behind in a tiny motel an hour outside of St. Louis.

"I told you to put the luggage in the car," Linda yelled at Laffit.

"It was your make-up case. I was taking care of the big suitcases. You couldn't take care of that little one?" he screamed back.

"We have to go back."

"Are you crazy? It's not gonna be there. Even if it were, the jewelry would be all gone by now. We're not going back."

"I'm calling the motel. What's the name of the place?"

Linda called and the man at the desk looked in the lost and found while Linda waited on the phone, drumming her nails on the small side table in their motel room.

"You do! Oh, thank you. We'll be back tomorrow to get it. Thank you. Thank you. I'm so relieved." Linda hung up the phone. "Laffit, they found it. We have to go back."

"I am not driving ten hours there and ten hours back," Laffit replied stubbornly.

Linda was not deterred. "You don't have to. We'll fly there and back."

Linda spent the next two hours finding out where the airport was, how to get to it, and what flights they could take in the morning. She also had to arrange for a rental car at the St. Louis airport so they could drive the sixty miles out of the city to where the motel was.

"This is a waste of time and money, I'm telling you," Laffit cautioned her. "You're going to be heartsick when you get there and you find out there's nothing in that case but cold cream."

Linda cried all through the night. "My engagement ring is in there. My wedding ring." With each item she remembered, she cried more. Laffit's anger with her began to dissipate when he saw how truly miserable she was.

"Don't worry, baby," was all he could say. "We'll go look. Maybe we'll get lucky."

They awoke at five thirty the next morning and drove forty-five minutes to the nearest airport where they caught the flight to St. Louis. Once in St. Louis, they picked up a rental car and drove to the motel. They arrived early afternoon and Linda strode purposefully to the front desk.

"Hi, are you James? I spoke to you yesterday. I'm Linda Pincay and I accidentally left my make-up case here yesterday morning."

"Oh, yes, let me go get it for you," the man said as he retreated into a door behind the desk. When he emerged a few minutes later, Linda exclaimed,

"That's it!" She eagerly took the small red case from the man.

Linda slid the latch to the right.

"Do you mean to tell me you didn't even lock that thing?" Laffit almost yelled.

She ignored him as she opened the case. The lid lifted and there inside were her lipsticks, her hairbrushes and tucked in the right corner, her green suede jewelry box. Linda opened it and there were her beloved treasures.

"They're here! They're here!" Linda squealed. She hugged Laffit, she shook the man's hand and gathered the bag.

"Come on, we've got a plane to catch. We'd better hurry up."

By the time they landed back in Oklahoma and drove back to the motel, Linda was feeling poorly. At first she thought it was the stress of the past twenty-four hours but when she awoke the following morning, it was clear she had come down with the Hong Kong flu. In the car, Laffit drove and Linda slept but by the time they made it to Texas, Laffit was beginning to feel sickly himself. That night they reached Amarillo and spent the next twenty-four hours in a motel drifting in and out of consciousness. The following day, both husband and wife felt well enough to travel again.

The surprise on that trip was not the found jewelry, as memorable as that was. The real gift was the pregnancy that was the result of that twenty-four hour stop in Amarillo. Sweatboxes, diet pills and extreme diets had been left behind when they got on the road; exactly what they suspected had interfered with their earlier attempts but couldn't know for certain.

As sick as they both were on that trip, they'd managed to make a baby. They were just a normal married couple, taking a road trip—albeit two pretty sick people, but people who were about to become parents for the first time.

Nine months to the day they checked into that Amarillo motel, baby Lisa was born.

DeGregory

CHAPTER 7

On September 7, 1969, Lisa Jean Pincay, six pounds, seven ounces, was born at Cedars Sinai hospital in Los Angeles ushering in a new chapter for Laffit and Linda. Both were perfectly suited to their new roles; they were family people at heart.

At the races, happily, things were equally stellar. Only one prize still eluded Laffit. He wanted to win the Kentucky Derby. In 1970 he finally rode but his horse, Unconscious, the five to two favorite, broke down during the race, coming in a disappointing fifth. It was a crushing blow for Laffit.

On a roll.

But that first Derby try was only a momentary disappointment. The year Lisa was born Laffit broke phenomenal records: He beat Shoemaker's record of 83 wins in a single meet at Santa Anita (Laffit brought in a whopping 138) and exceeded Johnny Longden's Hollywood Park record of 105 wins by one—Laffit earned 106 wins, a new record.[5]

---

[5] *Hollywood Park 2003 Media Guide.*

His new responsibilities renewed Laffit's commitment to riding, not that he needed any more incentive. In addition to a new baby, Laffit added another person to his world. He took on a new agent, a man who would transform Laffit from a successful jockey to a superstar rider.

Laffit had met jockey agent Vince DeGregory in New York at Aqueduct Racetrack. At that time, De Gregory was managing rider Angel Cordero, who hailed from Puerto Rico. Laffit was still being represented by Camillo Marin, but Laffit knew it was time for a change. Trainers and owners had been complaining to Laffit about Marin's behavior and everything he heard concerned him.

"I wanted to ride you on Belvedere, Laffit, but Marin never got back to me when I called."

"Laffit, I'm a little ticked at you. How come you were taken off my horse like that at the last minute? I had trouble finding another rider."

Decisions that Marin made deeply affected people's perceptions of Laffit, a jockey who wanted his reputation to be exemplary. The time had come for Laffit to move on.

Everyone in riding knew Vince DeGregory and knew what a magnificent job he had done with Angel Cordero's career. Sure, Cordero was an extraordinary talent, but DeGregory had brought out the best in him.

DeGregory was famous in the industry for his meticulous record keeping. The man was never without his little black book of statistics. He knew which horse won, by how many lengths, who the jockey was, who the trainer was, the kind of track the horse ran on. You name it, Vince knew it. There wasn't a thing about a rider, a horse, or a trainer that DeGregory didn't know. His system of placing a given rider on a specific horse, competing against a certain group of riders, was formed by his belief that a lot of knowledge goes a long way. Based on his results, he was right.

It was a friend who alerted DeGregory to Laffit's potential. "You should watch him, Vince, he's strong." So DeGregory kept Pincay in his peripheral vision and what he saw in the young Laffit was a diamond in the rough—a rider not fulfilling his potential—who could benefit from someone who could take him to the next level.

Laffit had been toying with the notion of moving beyond Marin when he heard that Cordero had chosen to stay in Florida and DeGregory was moving back to California. So he invited DeGregory to dinner.

Laffit, Linda and Vince had dinner with Dr. Ruben Marchosky and his wife at Hogan's Restaurant that fateful evening, a popular Arcadia spot. It was Linda who quizzed DeGregory with the important questions that night. DeGregory knew immediately that Linda was not your ordinary jockeys' wife. She was intensely interested in not only her husband's career, but in the business in general. And she was smart.

"What makes you think you can take Laffit to the same place you took Angel?" Linda wanted to know. DeGregory smiled. "Look, you asked *me* to dinner. I know what I can do for Laffit. The question is, can Laffit do what I *think* he can do?"

The question was left hanging between them. It had been quite a while since someone had challenged Laffit's abilities. For the past few years everyone was so impressed by what Laffit had achieved that no one imagined he could possibly reach even greater heights.

When dinner was over, the group retreated to the bar where live music played. The conversation turned back to Laffit and riding.

Finally De Gregory bluntly asked, "Do you want to beat Shoemaker as the leading rider or not?" The two couples laughed at the notion of anyone beating The Shoe but DeGregory didn't think the question was funny. In fact, he got angry. He stood up and threw down his precious black book. "If you don't think you're the best jockey in America then I don't want to work with you," De Gregory announced. "I have to go to Florida tomorrow for a few days. When I get back, you make up your mind. Do you want to be the best jockey who ever lived or not? " DeGregory then picked up his book and left. For a few minutes, everyone was stunned into silence.

De Gregory was not without prospects. Many riders had approached him, hoping for his guidance. Cordero had called from Florida repeatedly begging DeGregory to come south, even offering DeGregory a whopping thirty percent commission if he'd change his mind and come back. But

DeGregory had fallen in love with Southern California and something about Laffit—something intangible—appealed to him.

Horse racing is nothing if not a business filled with people with big dreams, who relish big triumphs. The agent and the jockey were two men with larger-than-life desires. But DeGregory felt it was Laffit who needed to make the leap of faith into his future, not the other way around. He was already a believer.

DeGregory knew he could make Laffit Pincay Jr. a superstar, but it would mean changing Laffit's thinking beyond being a great rider into believing he was a spectacular rider, a rider who could achieve superstar status, who could be the greatest rider of all time. But DeGregory believed that unless Laffit was fully committed mentally to major success, he could not achieve it.

DeGregory, for his part, overwhelmed and excited Laffit. He tapped into something Laffit had trouble defining. He thought the mere notion of beating Shoemaker (not in a single race but as leading rider) was impossible, even though it was his fervent prayer. Leading rider meant you won more races than anyone. Even saying he wanted to beat The Shoe sounded too boastful, arrogant even. Yet De Gregory had penetrated deep inside Laffit's psyche. And Laffit met the challenge. He decided he was going to try.

Before they agreed to work together formally, they decided on a trial run to see how the working relationship manifested. Unfortunately, as luck would have it, when they were set to begin DeGregory had a commitment to be out of town for a jockeys' ball. Before he left, however, the agent set up Laffit's mounts, using the alchemy of his statistics and numbers and calculations. At that time, Laffit was eleven races behind Shoe's record at Santa Anita. DeGregory wanted to not just meet that record but to surpass it. That would mean getting Laffit to accept the notion of beating his idol on a regular basis.

Each night DeGregory phoned in to find out how the day had gone. Linda answered the first day.

"How did our boy do today? "DeGregory asked.

"He won three."

"How many did Shoe win?"

There was a pause. "Uh, none."

DeGregory was delighted with the news. "I think tomorrow we're gonna have a big day." Laffit was due to ride Rising Market the next afternoon in a $75,000 purse race.

When DeGregory called the following evening it was Laffit who picked up the phone.

"So, how did it go today?"

"Oh we had a pretty good day." DeGregory learned early on that Laffit was not one to boast. He let his racing talk for him.

"How many did you win?"

"Five."

"Oh."

"And we won the stake's race, too."

"Great. How many did Shoe win?"

"None."

"That's the way to do it, Laffit, one race at a time. I told you, you can do this."

When DeGregory got back in town he phoned Laffit.

"Did you decide what you want to do? Do you think I can cut the mustard or do you want another agent?"

"Oh, no, no, I don't want another agent," Laffit quickly told him. Laffit had been renewed by DeGregory's belief in him, by his challenge, by his raising the bar to a place he hadn't imagined he could reach. Both sensed it was going to be a happy business marriage.

And it was. DeGregory called the right mounts and Laffit rode them splendidly. They both respected each other's talent and consequently, created racing magic. Neither questioned the other, both believing that it was in each man's best interest to do their respective jobs. DeGregory knew how to tout Laffit to the press; Laffit knew how to wow them on the track.

From the beginning, when it came to races, DeGregory wanted nothing left to chance. He insisted Laffit learn new skills, including how to handle the whip with both hands for greater flexibility, not an easy thing to master. He forced Laffit to learn how to change goggles with lightening speed—as many as seven pair—so that a muddy track would not impede the jockey on his road to victory. When one set of goggles grew caked with mud, they were quickly pulled down around the jockeys' neck and the new pair was flipped down from the top of the his helmet—all while controlling a horse as it raced around the track at fifty miles an hour. DeGregory proved right. These added skills (along with DeGregory's vast knowledge about each horse) and Laffit's new drive gave Laffit a competitive advantage other jockeys didn't have. He simply won more often.

Linda, Laffit and Vince DeGregory

"They were a show, Pincay and DeGregory, wherever they went. There was the glib, peripatetic DeGregory… movie-star suave and tall, engaging, very savvy … and there was Pincay, handsome and intense with high Indian cheekbones and black hair," said writer William Nack.[6]

That year, 1970, much to his own amazement, Laffit wound up beating Shoemaker's record. That same year, he was awarded the George Woolf Memorial Award, the award given to a rider whose career and personal conduct exemplifies the best of horse racing. Laffit had only been in the United States four years and already he had reached one of horse racing's highest pinnacles.

None of this was effortless. DeGregory knew better than anyone (anyone that is except Linda) the daily grind Pincay endured to be on top. After one dinner together during which DeGregory witnessed the drastic kind of diet Laffit was limited to, he declared he could never eat with the man again. It made him too guilt-ridden downing a T-bone steak while Laffit picked at a two-ounce piece of fish.

[6] "No Sweat for Laffit," William Nack, *Sports Illustrated*, October 29, 1979.

VooDoo

CHAPTER 8

Anxious the following season to race at Aqueduct against big name riders, Laffit began pressuring De Gregory about going to New York. Laffit wanted to be where the big money could be won. But DeGregory would have none of it.

"You can't go."

"Why not?"

"The truth? You're too heavy. Trainers aren't going to use you when they have lighter riders to choose from."

"What would I have to pull?"

"Those other riders are 112, 113 [pounds]."

"I can make that."

"Well, if you can," DeGregory reluctantly acceded, "then I guess we could go."

DeGregory wasn't so sure his strapping jockey could make the weight. He'd seen how little Laffit already ate. In fact, after the one and only dinner they shared together, he didn't know how Laffit had the strength to ride every day.

But Laffit was determined to go to New York and indeed, dropped three pounds. So off they went.

When they arrived in Saratoga, DeGregory's hometown, he moved into his father's house and moved Laffit and his family into a rental house next door. He then drove to the local Sears and purchased a personal sauna to put in the family room at Laffit's house. He hoped Laffit could sweat off the weight while he watched television. It worked. Laffit kept his weight down and went head to head with, among other people, DeGregory's ex-client, Angel Cordero.

Laffit won.

From 1970 to 1975 the duo of Pincay and DeGregory earned five consecutive national monetary championships, three Eclipse awards (racing's equivalent of the Oscar) and $18 million in purses.

All this success put Linda and Laffit in the position of being able to fulfill a dream. They wanted their own home, especially now that they had a two-year-old. Linda searched and found the perfect house on Los Grandes street in Los Feliz, an elegant Hollywood neighborhood crammed with history and celebrities (Cecil B. DeMille, Raymond Chandler, Al Jolson and Howard Hughes all lived in the Los Feliz area at one time). Laffit fell in love with the house and didn't hesitate to make an offer.

The house on the hill had two stories and a perfect view of the city of Los Angeles. It was particularly enchanting at night when lights twinkled in the distance. Linda relished decorating her new home and before long turned it into a showplace. They both enjoyed hosting birthday parties, card parties, barbecues, holiday gatherings, and swim parties—to which everyone was invited.

Linda also found a housekeeper, Luz Maria, who was wonderful with children and very hard-working. Best of all, she was someone who enjoyed entertaining their guests. Laffit could bring home a hungry crew of ten men at midnight and Luz Maria would cheerfully get up and cook for all of them.

Laffit's professional and domestic lives were thriving.

Linda and Laffit. This was a love match destined to last.

But as lovely as the Los Grandes house was, not everything that happened there was pleasant.

One day Linda answered a knock at the front door and found a tall, slender man with a long, gray beard. He was dressed all in black with a string bowtie like the type worn in the Old West. Over his right shoulder Linda could see a vintage black hearse.

"May I help you?" Linda asked.

The man replied in a slow, deep voice. "I'm here to pick up the remains of Linda Pincay."

A chill ran down Linda's spine. She instantly grabbed the heavy wooden door and slammed it shut in the man's face. She stood there for a few minutes, too shaken to move.

"Who was that?" Laffit asked, entering from the kitchen.

Linda told him what had happened.

Laffit laughed.

"What's so funny?" Linda wanted to know.

"Linda, this is a joke, don't you see?"

"A joke? Who would do something this sick as a joke?" Linda said, tears beginning to form. "I don't think it's a joke. It scared me."

When he saw that she was truly shaken, Laffit came over to his wife and hugged her.

"Baby, I'm sorry you got frightened. I shouldn't have laughed. Let's forget about it. You're right, it wasn't funny. It was stupid. Come on, let me get you a soda, okay?"

Within hours, both Laffit and Linda had moved past the incident.

That evening the phone rang.

"Is this the Linda that can promise me a good time?"

"What?" Linda asked, confused by the question.

"Someone gave me your number and said you know how to _____."

The words hit Linda like a fireball. She hung up the phone as though it were electrified. She ran to Laffit and told him about the call. This time he didn't laugh.

"What the hell is going on here?"

It was moments like these that Laffit was glad he kept a .22 and a .38 in the house for protection. Linda may have hated the guns—been terrified of them, in fact—but they were necessary, Laffit felt. Especially when crazy people began calling.

In the mail the next morning a box arrived addressed to Linda with no return address. Inside the box was a voodoo doll with pins stuck all over it. Linda shrieked when she saw it. At the track that same day, Laffit received disturbing, unsigned letters.

Who could be doing this? Neither Linda nor Laffit could come up with an answer. Friends were equally perplexed. They couldn't even suggest a possibility. The couple had no enemies, in fact, they were much loved.

Baffled by what was going on, Linda agreed to go with her sister to see a psychic, someone in Hollywood who was said to have remarkable powers. His name was Peter Herkos. Herkos had been recommended to Millie by actress Phyllis Davis. Millie was an old friend of Phyllis and Millie asked her to arrange an appointment for Linda.

In the meantime, the most frightening thing of all occurred. A social worker knocked on the door one morning saying there had been a report that Linda was abusing their daughter. Linda was stunned. The social worker insisted on immediately interviewing four-year-old Lisa. Afterward the woman told Linda, "I can see there's been no abuse here," to which Linda breathed a huge sigh of relief. Nonetheless, the stakes had been raised. Whoever it was who was doing this, was dangerous.

When she arrived for her session, Linda told Herkos all that had happened. Herkos wanted to see the letters and the voodoo doll, but unfortunately Laffit had already burned the doll. "Then bring me the pins from the doll," he said to her.

When Linda got home and told Laffit what Herkos needed, he meticulously went through the garbage and placed all the pins in a plastic bag. The next day she brought Herkos the pins, the letters, and, as instructed, a pair of Laffit's socks.

When Linda handed Herkos the socks, he slowly turned them over in his hands. He furrowed his brow. "What's wrong with this guy?" he asked. "Why doesn't he eat?"

Linda was mesmerized and wrote down every word Herkos said. "Mary." He said, then shook his head. "No, it's isn't Mary." He was having trouble coming up with the name. "I need to dream on this," he told Linda. "Call me tomorrow."

When she did, Herkos told her the name "Maria," he said. It was definitely Maria "This was a woman who knew your husband before you married him and she sees you having the good life she thinks should be hers."

Ten years earlier, before Laffit had met Linda, he had in fact dated a woman named Maria, but it was by no means a serious romance. He remembered, however, that when he told her he was getting married, she was quite distraught.

"You're too young to get married," she declared.

He never saw Maria after that.

Armed with a name, Laffit hired a private detective to track the woman down. After the man did, he reported to Laffit, "I guarantee you she's not going to bother you anymore." Laffit never asked what was said to the woman, he was just glad she was never heard from again.

Though the Maria problem ended, another arose that proved harder to resolve.

From the start, Linda was emotionally tied to the wins and to the losses. When Laffit won she was elated, when he lost she was depressed. Said one sports writer: "She is much like a celebrity politician's wife, fiercely loyal, totally involved, deadly certain that her man can do no wrong." [7] And while Laffit and Vince got along well, Linda and DeGregory began to clash.

Their disagreements came to the surface one day when Linda wanted her husband to ride one of her father's horses in an upcoming race. DeGregory had already committed Laffit to another horse and refused. DeGregory felt it was essential that he keep his word. Linda didn't agree. For her, family came first. Friction began to mount between rider, spouse, and agent with Laffit caught tightly between the two.

---

[7] "Pincay: Sweating to Be Superstar." Gordon Jones, *Los Angeles Herald Examiner*, February 24, 1974.

THE COLLAPSE

CHAPTER 9

The pressure to keep succeeding began to manifest in dangerous ways. During the late 1970s, though he swore he never would, Laffit began purging.

He certainly wasn't the only jockey engaging in the practice, but Laffit had resisted it for years; he found it disgusting.

It was, and still is, riding's dirty little secret. Jockeys know if they aren't slim—even the best of them—trainers will find lighter jockeys to ride their horses. As tacit proof that race-tracks support the practice, some jockey bathrooms are equipped with specially shaped oblong toilets, called heaving bowls, with grip bars for the express purpose of vomiting.[8]

The debate about weight has been waged for years. Most trainers and owners believe that the lighter the jockey, the less chance of injury to their costly investment, their horse. Jockeys, on the other hand, contend that a two-to-three-pound difference would have minimal consequence to horses and would create a healthier lifestyle for jockeys.

Each jockey room also has a sweatbox or steam room where jockeys go to sweat off pounds, a dangerous and potentially life-threatening exercise if overdone—a practice Laffit had engaged in for years.

Laffit's push to rank number one in money earned—and races won—became all-encompassing. DeGregory would coach him, chide him, and berate him.

"What the hell were you doing out there?"

"The horse—there was something wrong—he just gave up."

"I don't want to hear that. Why didn't you whip him?"

"I told you there was something wrong with him."

"You looked like a beginner. I was embarrassed."

His diet, his exercise routine, and his lifestyle all revolved around the track. If Laffit failed to win a coveted race, Linda and DeGregory's overt disappointment only added to his own.

---

[8] "Horse Racing's Dirty Little Secret," Neil Schmidt, *The Cincinnati Enquirer*, April 25, 2004.

But not every moment of Laffit's life was spent racing, though it sometimes felt like it to him. Thanks to some Hollywood friends and his celebrity status, in 1974 Laffit was invited to guest star as himself on the television show, "Rockford Files" with James Garner. The gig proved challenging for Laffit. Made to sit around all day on a dark

Though he had movie star looks, television wasn't for Laffit.

soundstage, Laffit fretted over properly delivering his one line. Though he did well, he decided that show business wasn't for him. It was on the track, not the silver screen, that he was happiest.

Sports writers sang his praises on a regular basis and Linda pressed the clippings in an album:

"He is everywhere. Backstretch, homestretch, winner's circle ... every place you look, there's that tiny, muscular Panamanian with the chiseled face and the straight black hair, preparing himself in every way he can to excel."[9]

Certainly Laffit's successes would not have come without his extraordinary, some say super-human, self-discipline. In

---

[9] "Laffit Pincay's Winning Touch," Dwight Chapin, *The Los Angeles Times*, June 28, 1974.

fact, his willpower was becoming legendary. Trainer D. Wayne Lukas told of riding on a plane with Laffit and watching as Laffit ate only half a peanut, his dinner, while other passengers ate full meals. Another time Laffit was spotted eating a single saltine cracker—but only after he'd brushed off all the salt.

Darrell Vienna, another trainer, tells the story of watching Laffit break from his remarkable self-restraint. Both men were on horse owners Joe and Julie Herrick's private jet heading from Los Angeles to a race at Pimlico racetrack near Baltimore when they heard a huge explosion. Laffit turned and saw one of the plane's engines burst into flames. Laffit held his Daily Racing Form tightly to his chest and as he looked around, he saw Vienna grabbing his heart. Someone began frantically looking for the exits, another passenger dragged out a rosary.

A very composed Mrs. Herrick then turned from her seat in front and in a calm voice announced, "I have just spoken to the pilot and there is nothing to worry about, this plane can fly all the way to Kansas on the one engine."

At which point Laffit threw down his paper and yelled, "Bullshit!"

When the plane put down at the next airport, Vienna watched Laffit scramble off the plane and run to a candy machine where he bought not one, but two candy bars which he immediately tore open and devoured. Vienna was laughing as Laffit screamed, "I came so close to dying I have to have this!"

For Laffit, it could only be a life or death event that would make him break from his normal discipline.

Linda could attest to the fact that she was living with a driven man and she supported that drive by supporting him. Her energies went toward making things easy for Laffit so he could concentrate completely on racing. Friends and family even knew not to call the Pincay house on Laffit's days off. Laffit was resting and that rest was essential.

What Laffit was doing—encouraged by Linda and by DeGregory—was working. His reputation, his skills, were growing. People shook their heads in disbelief at his feats.

And his drive to get even better at what he was doing was remarked upon by all who came in contact with him. Trainer Farrell Jones said, "I've seen him run back to the jockeys' quarters to see the rerun of the race and maybe learn something." [10] Laffit was never satisfied, never good enough, there was always more to learn.

Occasionally, people around him complained that Laffit seemed distant at times. But it wasn't a conscious aloofness, "I was constantly thinking, trying to figure out what I'd done wrong, what I could do better next time. I was always focused on the next race."

Keeping his energies focused kept Laffit evolving and winning.

The director of racing at Hollywood Park, Jimmy Kilroe said, "He has the strength of Arcaro, the judgment of Shoemaker, the determination of Longden, and the coolness

---

[10] Ibid.

of Woolf."[11]   In other words, he was the best of the best combined into one jockey. For Laffit, it was a joy and a burden all at once.

It was Bill Shoemaker who gave Laffit the greatest compliment of all, "If there's a better rider, I haven't seen him. He's the toughest I've ever faced." [12]

Celebrities were asked to be introduced to him: John Wayne, Greer Garson, Kirk Douglas, Jimmy Stewart, Robert Stack, Roy Rogers, Alfred Hitchcock. The fact that they knew who he was shocked Laffit. And when they praised his riding, it was almost more than the boy from Panama could handle.

But the glamorous life extracted a price. At the height of pushing himself, feeling his wife's ambitions for him, and compounded by the pressures from his agent, Pincay was forced off his mount when he collapsed after a session in the hotbox. At the time he told the press it was a reaction to a penicillin shot. His agent and Linda knew otherwise. He was pushing himself too hard. Rather than slowing down after the collapse, he continued to ride his scheduled horses for the next ten days, taking weight off every single day.

Then at Aquaduct, a few weeks later, Laffit became dizzy and weak. He was rushed to North Shore hospital where doctors determined that not only was Laffit badly dehydrated, he had almost no potassium in his system and was dangerously close to a heart attack. Doctor's told Linda that

---

[11] Ibid.

[12] Ibid.

she must get him to stop these dangerous practices immediately.

"The outlook is grim." One reporter declared, "Racing may have lost one of its greatest race riders, maybe the greatest rider of them all."[13]

The release from the hospital didn't end the drama. Though the intravenous feedings fed his body, Laffit's psyche needed an infusion as well. The jockey finally had to acknowledge to himself that he was drained physically *and* emotionally.

The past months had been hard not only on Laffit but on Linda as well. Living with his precarious health, his relentless drive, and his volatile moods was becoming exceedingly difficult for Linda.

The reality of how a jockey keeps his weight under control on a daily basis affects those who live with him. The lack of nutrition contributed to Laffit's dangerous health situation and his mental brittleness. He not only had no physical fat upon which to draw, he was without mental cushioning as well.

Adding to this was the fact that for the past few years Laffit had taken various forms of diet pills: Dexamil, Escatrol, Desbutal and amphetamines, all of which worked for a short period of time, then didn't. The pills may have helped him lose weight but they also altered his personality. He developed a short fuse, especially at home. Linda gently sug-

---

[13] "Pincay Losing Battle of the Bulge," Gene Ward, *The Los Angeles Times*, October 29, 1974.

gested one day when he was particularly moody that "That's not you, Laffit. It's the pills." (Knowing Linda was right, he quit taking them altogether in 1975, shortly before the FDA removed them from the market. But it took a year before he began to feel he'd truly broken the addiction.)

Clearly, Laffit was stressing his body in multiple ways. The effects of purging alone on an average person's body are various and the longer one engages in the activity, the more complications can develop. Heart attacks, kidney failure, ruptured esophagus, gastrointestinal bleeding, tooth loss, hair loss, nerve damage, not to mention outright death, are all possibilities[14].

In 2000, twenty-nine-year-old jockey Chris McKenzie died after suffering a heart arrhythmia when his potassium levels plummeted, almost exactly what had happened to Laffit. That same year Chris Antley, a two-time Kentucky Derby winner, died of what was listed as an accidental overdose of drugs used as appetite suppressants.[15]

The purging, the over-exercising, the extreme dieting, the sweatbox and the pills created a lethal cocktail Laffit did not know how to give up.

He desperately needed a break but none was scheduled. Then, in October of 1974, on his way home to California, Laffit's normal nervousness about flying suddenly turned

---

[14] "Bulimia Nervosa," Complications, *Mayo Clinic*, *www.mayoclinic.com*, June, 22, 2007.
[15] "The Jockeys' Guild History 1940-2000," *Jockeys' Guild*, *www.jockeysguild.com.*, June 13, 2007.

into terror. His palms grew sweaty, his vision blurry, he felt like he might vomit and he desperately wanted to bolt. Somehow, he made it safely home but once there he developed a terror of the sweatbox; the medicinal smell made Laffit physically ill.

Laffit had hit a wall. He was finally persuaded to take a two-month hiatus. Though it was a tough— almost impossible—decision, he knew he had to forgo racing records if he wanted to stay alive. And for the first time ever, clearly scared of his own failing health, Laffit agreed to rest.

That December a promotional excursion for track people had been planned and he and Linda traveled to Aruba with best friends Alvaro Pineda and his wife Donna, and the DeGregorys. The timing was perfect. Laffit was able to get away and simply relax.

The trip also allowed for some meaningful conversations. Pineda advised his friend to go easier on himself, that life was too short. In private, Linda confessed that she thought DeGregory—though she knew he meant well—was pushing him too hard.

Laffit came back from Aruba feeling a bit more stable and upon his return, consulted with a doctor who determined that the jockey was anemic and placed him on a high protein diet. He reported to the press that he was feeling better than ever. But in truth, he wasn't. Laffit was scared.

Though DeGregory clearly cared about the man, he had nonetheless been working Laffit hard. DeGregory saw it as the only option available if Laffit wanted to stay on top.

From the beginning, DeGregory's goal was to establish Laffit as the greatest rider of all time. He firmly believed in Laffit's potential and wanted it fully exploited.

At Hollywood Park. Linda in scarf, Donna Pineda across the table from her

Though Laffit had done remarkably well before joining DeGregory, the agent was the person who pushed the athlete further up the success ladder.

In many ways though, Laffit didn't need his agent to place greater expectations on him. By nature, he demanded the best from himself, every time, all the time.

On January 18, 1975, while Laffit was in the jock's room at Santa Anita preparing for the eighth race, they heard Chick Anderson, the announcer at Santa Anita, come over the speaker box. "There has been a terrible accident at the starting post. A jockey is down." All the jockeys scrambled to the monitor to see what was going on, but it was hard to make out who was injured and what kind of injury it was. The ambulance was there in a matter of seconds and paramedics were on the ground leaning over the fallen jockey. A few minutes later Anderson announced that Austin Mittler, the horse in question, had reared up causing the injury. The rider had fallen to the ground and was dead.

The rider, it turned out, was Alvaro Pineda.

A pall settled over Santa Anita Racetrack.

In the jockeys' room, there was disbelief. Fifteen minutes ago Pineda was *just there* joking with the others as he strode out of the room. The night before, he and

Alvaro Pineda.

Donna had been over to Laffit's house and Linda had cooked steaks for all of them. Afterward they'd played cards and Alvaro had won. Now he was dead. It was incomprehensible.

When Jacinto Vasquez, another jockey in the race, got back to the room he told the shocked group what he had seen. As the horses were being lined up into the stalls, Austin Mittler was restless and began bucking. Some have said that sitting on a horse in the gate is like sitting on a stick of dynamite. It was certainly true that day. Pineda stepped off the horse and onto the slender metal ledge on the side of the stall, hoping to stay clear of the wild animal but the minute he stepped off, the horse reared up and his powerful neck struck Pineda's head and sent it against the metal rail behind him. When Vasquez saw him on the ground he saw that Pineda was bleeding from his ears. He didn't have a chance, Vasquez told them.

Laffit ran to the phone and called Linda to tell her the news. But Linda has been watching the tragedy unfold on the television. She was as stunned as Laffit.

Every jockey and his family know the inherent dangers of racing. But the only way to go to work each day is to be aware of the possibility and then bury the fear as far back in your mind as possible. Injuries are a given, but death is a price no one expects to pay.

Most accidents happen during a race, which is why an ambulance trails riders from the moment each one begins.

The hope is that immediate care will minimize injuries. But *before* a race, or *after?* These are situations no one expects and why everyone that day was so stunned.

All jockeys—indeed anyone associated with racing—know that when you deal with live animals, anything can happen at any time. That day the point was driven home in a very painful, personal way.

Laffit gave his mounts to other riders that afternoon and he and Linda rushed to Donna's house. Suddenly weight problems, hotboxes and records paled in comparison to what had befallen the Pineda family. Donna was now a widow with two young children.

In a bitter twist of irony, the previous year Pineda had been awarded the George Woolf Memorial award for Outstanding Jockey. George Woolf, as it happened, was the last person killed on Santa Anita's racetrack. Now Pineda had joined him in a bizarre set of circumstances.

Riding is a daily gamble with the fates. Horse racing lost twenty-four jockeys during races in the 1970s, despite safety helmets, protective vests, better tracks and strict riding regulations.[16] But this wasn't any jockey that tragedy had befallen (not that one is more important than another). This was one of Laffit's closest friends. To make matters worse, Laffit felt personally to blame for the accident.

---

[16] "Jockeys' Guild History 1940-2000, " *Jockeys' Guild, www.jockeysguild.com*, June 13. 2007.

Pineda and Pincay were neck and neck at Santa Anita that year in the race to be lead rider. The rivalry was friendly but fierce. They admired one another's riding skills. Laffit also admired Alvaro for his successful battle against alcohol addiction.

Four days before his fatal accident, the two men had ridden in a race in which Pineda bothered Laffit's horse so badly, Pincay was forced to stand up on his mount to prevent an accident. After the race, the stewards called Pineda in. Pineda did not want to be suspended and begged Laffit, out of friendship, to go in and defend him—to lie for him. Laffit was torn but ultimately told the stewards it was merely an accident and Pineda got a pass. Pineda was extremely grateful to Laffit that day.

But if Laffit hadn't lied for his friend, if Pineda had gotten the suspension he should have, he would not have been riding that tragic day, and he would *not* have died. To this day, it haunts Laffit.

The depression that followed Pineda's death was crippling. Back at the track, Laffit became belligerent and was suspended several times for brawling and careless riding. That March he broke his collarbone when he flew over the head of his horse, El Sheeram. The break, ironically, proved a blessing because in the hospital doctors discovered a parasite in his blood that was sapping him of all energy. The virus, Toxoplasma Gondii, masquerades as the flu and is generally found in those with extremely weakened immune systems, certainly something that had plagued Laffit. The disease has been known to alter personalities and in rare cases, can be fatal. The parasite had found its way into Laffit's spleen which, thanks to his breaking his collarbone, the doctors discovered.

His altered personality was not only evident with his outbursts at the track, but at home as well. Linda Pincay told *Sports Illustrated* that year: "He was quiet and moody. There was no closeness—he was like a robot."[17]

After the hospital stay Laffit began to feel somewhat better. For a while he added vitamins to his regimen but found they added weight so he stopped taking them.

Happily, in 1975, Laffit was notified that he was being inducted into the Racing Hall of Fame, the youngest jockey ever to be tapped. It was a major honor, but Laffit had mixed emotions about going to the black tie affair. Part of him was thrilled to receive the prestigious award. Another part was terrified of speaking in front of a large group of people; he felt his English still needed improving. When he broke his collarbone in a race just weeks before the event and doctors advised against flying, Laffit was relieved. In his stead, he asked DeGregory to accept the award for him. So DeGregory donned his tuxedo and accepted the award and it was his smiling face that graced the sports pages the next day.

Linda was not happy.

---

[17] "No Sweat for Laffit," William Mack, *Sports Illustrated*, October 29, 1979.

Laffit continued to ride and continued to struggle with weight. Unfortunately the struggle was not in private. Despite his Hall of Fame achievement, *Newsday* magazine sounded a sour note in October: "The end of the Pincay dynasty may be near. The problems of weight pursues him daily ... plainly he's tired of it."[18]

As hard as he was trying, as much winning as he was doing, the problems were evident to all around him. The problem was, how to fix things?

Thanks to a week's suspension, Linda and Laffit decided to take a much needed vacation to Hawaii. It was time to reassess what was happening and what lay ahead.

One thing was certain, Laffit couldn't handle any more stress.

In Hawaii the couple had a chance to finally discuss something that had been on Linda's mind for quite a while.

"Laffit, I know Vince wants what's best for your career but I don't think he knows what's best for you as a person. He doesn't live with you. I do. It's too much. You'll kill yourself if you keep up this pace. It's time to slow down."

"He won't let me slow down."

"It's not a matter of what Vince will let you do, it's what you chose to do."

"What are you saying?"

---

[18] "Laffit Pincay: First With the Most," Bill Mack, *Newsday*, October 12, 1975.

"Maybe it's time for you to try a different agent."

It wasn't the first time Linda had broached the topic of firing DeGregory. In the past, Laffit had rebuffed any comments from Linda about Vince. This time though, he listened. He had to.

For a few days he mulled the idea over. When it was clear that it was the only move to make, he called his business manager and told him to fire Vince.

He didn't have the heart to do it himself.

TALK OF THE TOWN

CHAPTER 10

The table where Linda held court in the Turf Club (often accompanied by Millie and Roseann), was increasingly placed in a more prominent position until finally it was 'her table' and everyone knew where to find her on a Saturday afternoon. Lunch, a few drinks, some laughter and your husband winning—what could be more fun?

"Where's everyone meeting tonight?" was the question of the day when friends stopped by the table. As Laffit's successes grew, so did the status of the people who dropped by. Burt Bacharach and wife Angie Dickenson came often as did John Forsythe, Tim Conway, and a host of celebrity horse racing fans.

After the races, everyone repaired to a few regular hangouts: The Derby, Talk of the Town, Chasen's, Yamato's, Matteo's and of course, The Westerner. While jockeys showered, their wives and girlfriends hightailed it to the evening's designated spot and grabbed a table or waited at the bar for their heroes to arrive.

The racing crowd has an eclectic group of supporters. Besides wives and girlfriends, any number of agents, trainers, and owners stopped by the chosen venue to review the day's races.

One particular Saturday when Linda had been at the track with Millie, Roseann and Naila and Bob Winfield, Laffit agreed to meet up with the group at The Westerner, the closest and most convenient hangout near the track.

Linda stopped by the jockeys' room after the races to firm up the evening's plans. Laffit mentioned to Linda that some friends from Panama were at the races that day and he wanted to invite them for dinner. Linda's lack of response told him she didn't like the idea but neither said anything.

As Laffit showered and got dressed, his frustrations began to mount. Linda had spent all day with her friends, why couldn't they spend the evening with his? He'd just had another rough week dieting, working out, and going to the track each morning to work with the horses. He'd spent afternoons in the sweatbox, plus ridden hard in six or seven races every day. He deserved one night out doing what he wanted to do!

By the time Laffit arrived at The Westerner his mind was made up. He went to the bar and found Linda, sipping her usual—V.O. and water—sharing a laugh with Roseann.

"We need to talk," he told her.

She turned her barstool slowly and looked her husband in the eye.

"What about?"

"I'm getting tired of the fact that every time I want to bring my friends around, you don't like them."

"Look Laffit, if you want to see them so badly, fine. Go see them. I'm going home."

"Fine."

"Fine."

With that, Linda turned to her sister and Roseann and said, "Let's get out of here."

After the women left, Laffit chatted with some people he knew then went to Talk of the Town where he'd told his friends to meet him. When he walked in, he spotted Linda sitting at the bar. She was laughing and having an animated conversation with Laz Barrera, the trainer. Roseann and Millie were at the bar also.

Laffit quickly strode up to Linda.

"I thought you were going home."

"Well, I changed my mind."

"How much have you had to drink?"

"None of your business."

"You were drinking all afternoon, weren't you?"

Roseann and Millie exchanged looks.

"Why did you tell me you were going home if you weren't?"

"I told you, I decided not to."

"So you lied to me."

"I said I changed my mind."

"Go home."

Linda pushed her face in front of Laffit's, defying him.

"Make me," she said in a slow, deliberate tone. Laffit was livid. He grabbed Linda's face and twisted it to the right.

Linda flailed her arms to get away from her husband's grip, then started to hit his arm. Laffit grabbed her hair. She grabbed Laffit's hair.

Barrera jumped in, "Hey, calm down, Laffit."

Roseann joined the fray, stepping up to Linda and Laffit. "What the hell is wrong with you, Laffit?"

Laffit then twisted Roseann's face away just as he had Linda's.

"Stop it, stop it," Linda screamed. Everyone in the bar was looking. Linda fled to the ladies room, crying.

Laffit stormed out of the restaurant.

It was not the first time that arguments between the two had turned physical. The first time was a verbal fight in their living room in which they traded abuses. Laffit was ready to blow.

"Go ahead, hit me!" Linda taunted. "Hit me! I know you want to. I'll pick up this phone and call the police. Don't think I won't."

Laffit took a step closer; they were now chin to chin.

"What? Too chicken?"

Laffit raised his hand and struck Linda on her left cheek.

The surprise in her eyes, the fear, and the pain, was instantaneous.

Linda then turned, eyes brimming with tears, and retreated to their bedroom. Laffit stood there, devastated. He was instantly remorseful. How could he have done that? He wished she *would* call the police, that he would be hauled away and punished for what he had done.

Somehow both had begun a dance of destruction which neither enjoyed, but which neither seemed capable of ending.

Since Linda's first suicide attempt, the couple's fights escalated more quickly, more ferociously. Each had a temper. Laffit was moody, Linda was depressed. They would patch things up, things would fall apart.

Drained by the constant fights, Laffit calmly asked Linda at one point if perhaps they should separate, since neither seemed happy. Linda cried. She told him she'd surely kill herself if he ever left her. So he stayed and the emotional roller coaster dipped low and rode high, depending on the day, on each person's mood, and on how the races had gone that particular day.

Nonetheless, pressures mounted. Laffit's work affected both of them and the way each wanted to spend their evenings did not seem to mesh. Linda liked her coterie of girlfriends, Laffit preferred his Latin buddies.

The night he had stormed out of Talk of the Town, Laffit came home at two in the morning after having dinner with his Panamanian friends. The light into the bedroom was on which surprised Laffit as he thought Linda would be asleep by then.

What he found in the bedroom terrified him. There on the bed, with bedclothes pushed roughly aside, was Linda, fully clothed. Her arms were in an awkward position above her head and her eyes were half open. He knew immediately that she had overdosed. He frantically ran to the neighbor's house, pounding on their door, practically breaking it down, "Help me, help me, please."

Laffit had not believed that Linda would ever try suicide again; he had relied on Linda's devotion to their little girl as security. Having been so devastated by the loss of her own mother at an early age, Laffit couldn't imagine Linda inflicting the same pain on Lisa.

The paramedics brought Linda to Arcadia Methodist Hospital. Her stomach was pumped and she was quickly out of danger. The doctors recommended that she remain and have psychiatric counseling, but she adamantly refused. "There's nothing wrong with me!" she cried, and went home the next day.

Again, Linda didn't want to discuss the issue and again, Laffit didn't pursue it.

The next day, an announcer who had been at Talk of the Town the night before put a blind piece on his radio show, "What famous jockey was seen slapping his wife last night at a well-known jockey hangout? We'll tell you tomorrow." Luckily someone got to the reporter and the humiliating follow-up was never aired.

Despite the enormous worry over his wife and child, Laffit managed to stay focused on racing and winning, which he did with remarkable regularity. His ability to shut everything out but the race ahead of him was probably his saving grace and the thing that infuriated those around him who didn't have the same capability.

When he was riding well, Linda was happy and things seemed good. There were enough good days to keep the couple afloat. This was, after all, a love match. It may have been ill-fated but anyone who ever met them knew there was tremendous passion between Linda and Laffit. There was a genuine bond they shared that superseded everything else. When things were good they were very, very good. But when they were bad …

A short time later, Linda's dream house on Cummings Way went on the market. It was an elegant home just down the hill from their current place. The house was in pristine condition, larger than the Los Grandes one with a bigger pool plus a huge yard filled with mature fruit trees.

"Oh, Laffit, I love this house, love it. Please won't you just take a look at it? Please?"

Linda's pleadings were so sweet, Laffit knew he would be buying the house before he even stepped foot into it. But he was happy to bring Linda such joy and so they moved to the Cummings' house. Marge Everett gave them a dog, a Golden Retriever they christened Eclipse, as a house warming gift.

The family spent seven years in that house. They were not all happy ones.

WISH FULFILLED

CHAPTER 11

Angel Cordero and Jorge Valesquez were great compatriots of Laffit's. Talented riders, fellow Panamanians with great senses of humor, they were also fierce rivals who enjoyed racing against one another to see who'd come out on top in any given race. All notions of friendship stopped the moment the gates were opened and the race was on.

Laffit was set to ride against his friends, his first race after a ten-day suspension. During the suspension Laffit did something unusual—he stopped his normal routine. He simply relaxed. Getting back after those ten days off, however, Laffit was forced to seriously pay the piper. Ten days of limited exercise, little reducing, and only semi-dieting meant a brutal re-entry to work.

His first race back, Laffit got to the jock's room early. Knowing he had to pull off a lot of weight in a short amount of time, he took water pills and diet pills and stayed in the sweatbox from eight thirty in the morning until one in the afternoon. He lost six pounds in four hours. Eating that day, what little he did of it, was followed by flipping (vomiting).

As the three men sat mounted on their horses at the gate waiting for the race to begin, Jorge and Angel made fun of Laffit. Though Laffit wasn't exactly sliding off his saddle, he was so weakened by what he'd just put his body through, he had trouble staying upright.

They each vowed to best the other that day.

"I'm gonna whop you out there."

"Oh no you're not."

"I'm gonna beat both of you."

Being the worthy competitors they were, they knew it would be an all-out effort by each of them.

From the moment the gates opened, the race turned out to be as exciting as Laffit had anticipated—and as fierce. The three jockeys wove ahead and behind one another the entire race, leaving all other competitors in their wake. Laffit was tightly jammed between Jorge and Angel as they came into the home stretch, each man driving his horse as hard as he could in order to get ahead.

Just as they crossed the wire, the three horses momentarily collided but Laffit was certain his horse, Canyon, had won. The minute the race was over, both Angel and Jorge began yelling at Laffit, "We're going to claim foul! You bumped our horses."

Laffit thought about telling them to go f*** themselves but he simply didn't have the energy. It took everything he had just to stay in the saddle. The race had sapped what little reserves Laffit had left. Canyon was lead to the winners' circle but just as they reached it, the tote board began to blink. The stewards were calling for an inquiry.

How Laffit managed to walk to the stewards office that day, perhaps a half a mile away, is a mystery but once he got there he was so weak they immediately placed him in a wheelchair. Laffit could barely talk—let alone defend himself. Rather than conduct the inquiry, the stewards insisted Laffit be taken to first aid where they made him lie down and administered smelling salts. He instantly fell asleep.

When he awoke a short time later, his horse was declared the winner.

To this day, and with great good humor, Angel teases him about that win. "You owe me for that race you stole from me! And I want interest on those winnings!"

As the fates would have it, something delightful came out of the ten-day suspension that preceded this crazy race. Because Laffit simply relaxed and didn't adhere to his rigid routine during that break, he managed to get Linda pregnant—Laffit III was on his way!

Namesake

Chapter 12

Before leaving for Puerto Rico all those years ago—and the grand adventure that only he knew he was planning—Laffit had been introduced to a pretty young woman named Nina. Nina was brought to Laffit's house one evening after she begged his cousin Hector to be introduced to him.

Ever since Laffit became a local celebrity, Laffit was the object of women's attention. Barely eighteen, and being a normal young man, he had a healthy sex drive and was naturally flattered by Nina's interest. Even after Laffit informed her that he had signed a contract with Fred Hooper, and would be leaving for the United States as soon as his residency papers arrived, the girl was undeterred.

As far as Laffit was concerned, the relationship never truly got off the ground. Laffit was too focused on his future, on preparing to leave. Four dates was all they had. The couple dated twice and on their third and fourth date, had sex.

As he was packing for the U.S., the girl told Laffit she was pregnant. Laffit was baffled. Clearly it was possible, but she knew so soon? The fact that he didn't know much about her added to some genuine misgivings he had about her sudden announcement.

Though jockeys sexually perform normally, because of the various ways they stress their bodies, they often do not produce sperm in the way that an unstressed male's body does. So when Laffit confided the news of the girl's pregnancy to a few friends, they too had reservations. "You'd better be careful, Laffit. Some women are only after your money. Are you sure you're the only guy she's been with?" He honestly didn't know.

In Panama City at that time, blood tests to determine paternity were unheard of. The girl claimed Laffit had gotten her pregnant and there was no way for him to prove otherwise. Nina didn't push the issue after first mentioning it and Laffit continued with his plans to go to America.

Months later, after Laffit was in the States, a baby boy was born, and via friends, Laffit was sent pictures. Nina had not asked Laffit for his address when he left Panama and he had not offered it.

Blass Bescieu, Laffit's best friend in Panama, knew both Nina and Laffit and it was Blass that Nina confided in. She sought Bescieu's counsel so often that the girl's father came to Bescieu one day and confronted him about being the baby's father. For whatever reason, Nina had not initially named Laffit as the father to her family.

Some friends in Panama said the baby looked like Laffit but as Laffit stared at the photos he couldn't see any resemblance. Nina then began telling people that Laffit was the father of her baby, so it became accepted as public knowledge. But for years nothing more was said by anyone to Laffit about the issue.

While Linda and Laffit were dating he told her that there was a possibility that he had fathered a child in Panama. Since there was no contact with the mother, it became a non-issue for the couple.

Due to his extraordinarily busy schedule, it was a very rare occurrence for Laffit to visit Panama. When Laffit finally visited—his first trip in years—the four-year-old child's picture coincidentally appeared in the Panama paper, mentioning his birthday and who his parents were, stating Laffit was the father. Laffit suddenly felt badly. After all, there was the possibility that the child could be his so he contacted the boy's mother and told her he would officially recognize him. Nina said she wanted some financial support and Laffit agreed. Things went well until she told him she was going to name the boy after him.

When Linda heard that the girl wanted to name the child Laffit Pincay III, she put her foot down firmly. That name was reserved for their son, and *their* son only, with the sincere hope they would one day have one. The couple had been trying but to no avail. Nina's demand was a deal-breaker as far as Linda was concerned. If the mother wanted the last name and the financial support that would come with Laffit publicly acknowledging the boy, then she would have to relent on this name. Nina reluctantly agreed. She chose Alejandro, Laffit's middle name.

Though Laffit acknowledged the child, and paid for his care, he still harbored doubts fueled by rumors passed on to him from those in Panama. Consequently, the doubt and his busy schedule meant the child was well cared for but little seen by Laffit.

When he did finally see Alejandro again the boy was almost fifteen years-old and resentful of what he perceived was an absentee father. Laffit felt badly but explained to Alejandro that his career made him extremely busy and if he had more contact with him it would result in his wife divorcing him.

The boy's mother had married so the child had grown up with a father in the house, much as Laffit had when Rosario remarried. Laffit had done well with his own stepfather; he hoped Alejandro would do well with his.

Laffit had met his own father, the Venezuelan jockey, when he was five-years-old and then again at eighteen. His father came to Panama when Laffit was a youngster and all he remembers of the visit was his father spanking his behind when he crossed the street without looking.

The next time he saw the man was when he had been sus-pended from riding and the trainer, to make a point, flew his father over to replace him. Laffit enjoyed meeting and hav-ing a meal with him, but cer-tainly didn't feel connected to him in any way. If anything, su-per-disciplined Laffit felt his father didn't take proper care of himself.

Laffit Pincay Sr.

It would be another fifteen years before Laffit would see him again. His father came to stay with him and Linda when they were living in Los Feliz. Laffit tried to fix up his di-vorced father and his widowed mother, but the rematch didn't take.

After that visit, connections with his father were spotty at best. The last Laffit heard from his dad was when he wanted Laffit to invest in restaurants he and his sons were interested in. Laffit passed.

Many years later, Laffit went to a party in Panama for jockey Alexis Solis, to which he invited Alejandro, by now a young man. He never responded to the invitation and didn't show up for the party.

At one thirty in the morning, after the party, however, Laffit received a phone call from Alejandro. He was in the hotel lobby where Laffit was staying. He asked Laffit to come down immediately and see him. Laffit, deep into sleep, asked if they could meet the following day—but the young man hung up and never called again.

Several years later, Laffit heard from Alejandro's wife saying they had a little boy who unfortunately had heart trouble. Though Alejandro and his wife were no longer together, Laffit paid to send the child to Cuba for open-heart surgery, which thankfully was successful.

For a man so devoted to family, this was clearly an awkward chapter in his life. He decided to recognize Alejandro because he felt it was the right thing to do, even if he might have been the wrong man.

Linda and Laffit's much wanted son, Laffit Pincay III, was born December 8, 1975.

AGAIN

CHAPTER 13

I t was years before Linda attempted suicide again. Young Laffit was a baby when the third attempt happened after yet another fight. Again, Linda overdosed on pills. And again, Laffit found her.

"911? My wife has taken an overdose of sleeping pills."

When her friend Roseann came to see her in the hospital, Linda confided, "Laffit hates me."

"That's not true, sweetie," Roseann assured her, trying her best to soothe her friend.

"Oh Roseann, I can't live with him and I can't live without him," Linda cried.

Privately, all who knew and loved Linda were gravely concerned about her multiple attempts at suicide. All, it appeared, except Linda's father who never wanted to discuss the issue. But then, suicide was a painful topic for Bill Radkovich.

Linda told Laffit early on about her mother, how she had committed suicide when Linda was twelve years of age, how she had been the one to discover her, and how devastating it had been for her and for the family. Some years later, Linda's sister Maureen, not quite twenty, also died of a pill overdose. "It was the way that our family dealt with depression," Laffit's grown daughter Lisa would say years later.

Over and over Linda told Laffit and Roseann that she would die young "Not by suicide," she'd claim, "but by cancer or something."

She swore to her sister Millie that she would never commit suicide. And of course, she promised Laffit she wouldn't, on a regular basis.

She told Roseann, "How could I do that to my children?"

And now Linda had tried three times.

It was a dangerous game of Russian roulette and each time Linda's chances for success grew frighteningly higher.

Friends and family argued back and forth:

"It wasn't a real attempt or she'd have succeeded."

"What are you talking about? What if Laffit hadn't come home when he did?"

No one had any idea what to do but they all knew Linda needed help. They begged her to get it. "I don't need any," was all she'd ever say.

This last time, however, Marge Everett asked the hospital to send in a therapist to speak to Linda. Whether it was the wrong person or that Linda was just not receptive, Linda hated the man and refused to see him again, despite everyone's pleadings.

During the ride home from the hospital Linda sobbed, begging Laffit's forgiveness. By now Laffit was emotionally drained and deeply worried. He told Linda he loved her, but he didn't know how much more of this he could take.

"I promise you," she told him through tears, "this will never happen again. I hate that I do this, I don't know why I'm doing it. Don't worry, though, I will never do this to my kids again."

Tragically, Linda's problems were larger than either of them realized. She was making promises that day she was incapable of keeping. And he believed her because he simply didn't know what else to do.

THE GREATEST RACE

CHAPTER 14

I t was billed as the race of the century. The two greatest horses in the world ridden by two of the best jockeys of all times—Bill Shoemaker on Spectacular Bid versus Laffit Pincay Jr. on Affirmed. It was October 6, 1979, the Jockey Club Gold Cup Invitational, and racing fans went wild in anticipation. As high as the stakes were that day ($225,000, a princely sum in '79) it was a ride for pride, a ride for bragging rights.

Record crowds packed Belmont Park in New York. The rivalry was fierce, played out in a way that only sports fans can understand. Fans wore "team" t-shirts with their favorite horses names emblazoned in front. Blue and black shirts were for the Spectacular Bid fans and flamingo and black for Affirmed's fans. Supporters were uproariously vocal, well before the race began. The air was electric with anticipation.

That the race even took place was a marvel, and a testimony to the great sportsmanship of the horses' two owners. Louis Wolfson took understandable pride in his beloved Affirmed and Harry Meyerhoff had tremendous faith in Spectacular Bid. As both knew, a race of this nature carried huge risks.

A high-ranked horse can be gravely injured in a race such as this when going against a fierce competitor. With the wrong injury, a horse would not be able to race again or stand at stud, a crushing financial loss for owners. The point had been driven home a few years earlier when Ruffian broke down during a match race against Foolish Pleasure. When Ruffian had to be put down a pall settled over the entire racing industry. The 2008 Kentucky Derby win by Big Brown was eclipsed by the sudden collapse of runner-up Eight Belles a few feet after crossing the finish line, another brutal reminder of the fragility of race horses.

Both owners were taking a tremendous gamble.

Never in all his life was Laffit as nervous as he was this day, nor had he ever experienced as much pressure. He barely slept the night before. And he certainly didn't have sex. Laffit had learned earlier from other athletes the benefits of reserving all your energies—sexual ones included—when one had an important race.

He meditated the night before, seeing the race play like a movie in his head, re-editing bits and pieces along the way but the ending was always the same. He was the winner.

Reporters and photographers jammed the jockeys' room that afternoon. Neither Laffit nor Bill was given a moment to breathe once they arrived. Guards protected the entrance, and only those with the right credentials were allowed to enter. Inside, the noise in the room was overwhelming. Both jockeys were questioned and photographed by reporters and each signed programs, photos, and memorabilia. Family and friends, including a large contingency that had flown in from Panama, stopped by to wish Laffit luck.

When there were only twenty minutes to post time, the room was cleared of the crowd and each man, plus the two other jockeys competing that day, was left to prepare for the challenge ahead. Though other horses were in the race, everyone knew who this match was really between. Matching two seemingly perfect jockeys on equally perfect horses was what made this race so thrilling.

When they were finally called, Laffit, as usual, was the last to leave the jockeys' room. Because he got butterflies in his stomach before every race, he preferred less time in the paddock with owners and trainers who made him more nervous. Today was no exception.

He knew Linda was up in the clubhouse sitting at a table with Roseann and Millie and Cindy Shoemaker. Linda was in seventh heaven for this race. Laffit just hoped the event wouldn't be hard on Linda's friendship with Cindy. Somebody had to win, which meant one of the wives was going home with a loser that day. He certainly didn't intend for it to be Linda.

Laffit made sure his underwear was inside out and that the movie in his head now ran smoothly. He went over each move he'd make and was preparing for any eventuality that might occur on the track.

When he entered the paddock, Laffit was overwhelmed by the ferocity of the crowd. He'd never heard such a vocal group! They cheered when they saw Laffit mount the beautiful Affirmed.

Affirmed was not only a brilliant racehorse, he was a handsome one. He fulfilled a painter's image of what a

Affirmed looked like a painter's version of a racehorse

racehorse ought to look like. Spectacular Bid may have been

a great horse but his gray coat was dull in comparison to Affirmed's chestnut coat with the white markings on his nose.

Affirmed was led from the paddock through the tunnel toward the track. Laffit's heart began to pound heavily. As he emerged from the tunnel the roar from the crowd was as deafening as it was thrilling. This must have been what gladiators felt, he thought.

The horses moved into the gate without incident. Once there, Laffit was fully focused on the race. "Put his nose against the gate," he instructed the man. The crowd, the noise, the prize that lay ahead of him, was all dismissed from his mind. His total focus now was on Affirmed and bringing him across the finish line first.

The deep friendship between Laffit and Bill ended the minute any race began. They were professionals and as such, it was their job to emerge triumphant. Sitting atop his horse, Laffit said to himself, "Shoe, you may be one of my best friends but if I can mess with you today, I'm going to do it."

Both Shoemaker and Laffit broke strongly from the gate and as always, Affirmed took the lead. Laffit hoped Shoe would go inside, but not surprisingly, he didn't. He too knew the best part of the track was the outside.

Earlier, jockey friends Jorge Velasquez and Ange Cordero had warned Laffit to "go outside and stay there no matter what!" He had to keep Shoemaker on the inside and he concentrated on doing just that.

From the start, the four horses kept a tight rhythm going. Laffit worked hard to keep Shoemaker where he wanted him. Shoemaker attempted to move to the outside. Laffit could tell from furtive glances he made that the Shoe was hunkering down. He was not giving up and not about to be easily defeated. On the backside, Shoemaker came close to Laffit's right but Laffit purposely kept Affirimed outside to make it difficult for Shoe to go around. A few times Shoe tried to get even with Affirmed but Laffit kept his horse ahead of Spectacular Bid.

Laffit was living out the movie in his head and consequently could adjust to anything that Shoemaker did on that track. It was the advance of Coastal for which he had to stay alert, which was wise because out of the blue, suddenly Coastal was in second place but Laffit knew Coastal was no real threat.

Coastal held on going into the quarter turn, but once they rounded for home—as Laffit knew would happen—Affirmed flew by Coastal. Finally Shoe took Spectacular Bid to the inside and made a straight move forward. In the blink of an eye the battle was now between Affirmed and Spectacular Bid, exactly what the screaming fans wanted as they went into the stretch.

Laffit rode Affirmed hard, whipping him with his left hand, and the horse responded willingly. Then with one final push, Laffit urged Affirmed one length ahead of Spectacular Bid and whizzed across the finish line.

The crowd let out a roar. Laffit had just won the greatest race of the century!

As he was led to the winner's circle, he spotted Linda waving frantically at him. She was jumping up and down, clearly overjoyed. He waved back and she blew him a kiss.

The award was made, photos were taken, and the owners and trainers expressed how "tickled pink" they were.

Laffit was led to the pressroom where he met with reporters for more than an hour answering every last question. Finally he returned to the empty jockeys' room; the others had all gone home.

That night, friends celebrated Laffit's spectacular win with him and Linda at a steakhouse in Valley Steam. While others toasted his success with champagne, Laffit refrained. He had to race the next day.

Laffit and Bill never talked about the win, or the loss. That's not what jockeys do. They simply enjoy their victories, forget their failures, and look to the next race.

Horse racing is an admittedly glamorous sport, especially when you win a race like the one on Affirmed, but sometimes the underbelly of the gambling world that Laffit encountered was disturbing.

Laffit was asked many times to race internationally and did so but only when there was time in his schedule. Even the enormous purses that were offered him did not dissuade Laffit from his commitments in the United States where money titles were his goal. Nonetheless, when he did go abroad, the races and the trips proved exciting.

Laffit rode in many foreign places (Dubai, Tokyo, and Paris among others) but it was the Clasico Del Caribe in Venezuela that proved to be a particularly memorable race.

Laffit had been invited to Mexico to ride a horse called Lazerre in a qualifying race for the Clasico del Caribe which Lazerre won. The owner, a wealthy and powerful petroleum magnate, was delighted with the outcome and invited Laffit and his brother, Juan, to have dinner with him and some friends. The evening was great fun. The men laughed and drank and only became serious when the owner asked Laffit to ride the same horse in the Clasico, which was in a few weeks. Laffit explained that he'd love to but his agent had already committed him to another horse and therefore he couldn't.

"How about if I paid you $15,000?"

"Like I said, I'm already set."

"How much would it take?"

"I'm afraid there's no amount that could make me change my commitment."

Laffit was trying to be friendly and light-hearted but was beginning to feel pressure from the man.

The man left the room and returned with a stack of hundred-dollar bills. He plunked them on the table.

"How about $25,000?"

"Gosh, I feel terrible about this, but I just can't."

The man pulled out two more bundles from his jacket.

"What about $75,000?"

"I hate to have to do this, but my word is my word. I told this other owner he could count on me."

The man then leaned in and whispered, "Let me tell you something, my friend. If you don't ride my horse, then you're not riding any horse in that race."

Laffit's brother grabbed his arm and said, "We've got to go, Laffit. It's late." And they left.

"Do you want me to beat him up for you? I will." Juan said as soon as they were out of the room.

"Are you crazy? Forget about it. He's been drinking, that's all. Don't worry."

And nobody did until weeks later when Laffit went to the Venezuelan embassy to obtain his visa for the Clasico Del Caribe and was rudely denied it by the man at the front desk. "I don't have you down here," the man claimed.

Laffit was stunned. He knew the Venezuelan government had his name on the list of riders. He quickly suspected that the only thing that could have happened was that the owner of Lazerre had followed through on his threat.

Laffit went home and called Laz Barrera, the trainer of the horse he was set to ride. He explained what had happened and Barrera told him to stay put. An hour later, the trainer called back and told Laffit to report to the Venezuelan consulate tomorrow morning. If he was not given his visa at that time, Laffit was told, the person who refused to give it would be fired.

Laffit returned the next morning and was greeted by the same man he'd seen the day before. This time the man was obsequious. Laffit walked out within five minutes, visa in hand.

Laffit never asked Barrera who he knew or who he talked to. But he was disturbed by the string-pulling that was evinced by people with powerful connections.

In the end though, it was Laffit who was victorious. His horse won the Claico del Caribe and he never saw the owner of Lazerre again.

LANDALUCE

CHAPTER 15

O f all the horses Laffit was asked to ride in his long career, one of the best was Landaluce, the two-year-old daughter of Seattle Slew.

From the beginning, Laffit knew he'd found a remarkable horse. Landaluce's maiden race was run at Hollywood Park on July 3, 1982, with Laffit on board. The horse won easily. When the race was over and Laffit saw the time, he was incredulous. He asked trainer D. Wayne Lukas, "Is that the *real* time?" He couldn't believe the speed of the horse, a filly no less. In the racing world, the buzz was fast and genuine about Landaluce

One week after this uncommon horse won her debut race, she wowed the crowd at the Hollywood Lassie Stakes where she not only won by twenty-one unbelievable lengths but clocked in at 1:08 flat, a record time that has yet to be beaten.[19] At the Anokia Stakes race at Santa Anita she was such a sure thing, she was bet down to ten cents on the dollar. The horse won that race by eight lengths.

Landaluce went on to win every race she was in by lengths people couldn't remember seeing before. She won the Del Mar Debutante Stakes by six and one half lengths; the horse simply left everyone else in the dust.

The joy Laffit felt atop Landaluce was unrivaled. Donning the green silks with the white polka dots … it meant Laffit was about to win. He knew he had a champion horse, one that was destined to win the Kentucky Derby, the Preakness and the Belmont, the triumvirate of racing. Trainer Lukas felt the same way. He was certain the Triple Crown was theirs.

Her sixth eagerly anticipated race was sent for November 28, but six days earlier, the glorious daughter of Seattle Slew took ill with a viral infection. Her illness caught everyone off guard. Veterinarians tried valiantly but could not save Landaluce. The horse died with its head cradled in the lap of his loving trainer, Lukas, a man broken-hearted by the loss.

---

[19] "Slew was 1st Undefeated Triple Crown Winner," Lisette Hilton, *ESPN Classic*, November 19, 2003.

Laffit donned the green and white silks one last time and stood with tears in his eyes as they buried his beloved Landaluce in Hollywood Park.

The resulting depression may or may not have been the cause of the slump Laffit went into. Slumps are an inevitable part of racing—much the way injuries are—but for someone used to as much success as Laffit, this mental lock-down was almost impossible to adjust to or figure out.

The riddle was constant. You begin to lose races, you stop being asked to ride the better horse, therefore the harder it is to win because you are on an inferior horse. The harder you push yourself—or the horse, the more elusive the prize.

"This man is our Cal Ripken, Wayne Gretzky and Michael Jordan all rolled into 117 powerful Panamanian pounds."

Laffit dieted more, exercised aggressively, took whatever substance was legal to put in his body, and basically drove himself and those around him crazy. When you're in a slump, nothing works.

Tensions grew at home and neither Laffit nor Linda was happy.

The slump eventually ended, but it would take a Kentucky Derby win to break the spell.

MATTEO'S

CHAPTER 16

W hat Laffit hoped for was a night out with his wife. They had been at odds lately. As usual, he wanted to be with the Panamanian contingency, Linda wanted to be with her friends.

"Let's have a night out, just the two of us," Laffit offered. He made reservations at Matteo's in Beverly Hills, an elegant restaurant they both enjoyed.

They settled in at a cozy table and had just ordered their drinks when the front door opened and in came Roseann with Prince Amma. Immediately Laffit felt set up. The two women talked multiple times a day. There was no way each didn't know where the other was having dinner. Clearly Linda and Roseann had arranged this "chance" encounter.

Linda quickly invited the couple to join them for dinner. Laffit felt trapped and more importantly, betrayed. The Prince, who was from Arabia, owned horses that Laffit had ridden and though Laffit liked the man, this was not the intimate evening he'd had in mind. Laffit couldn't refuse to have them join them and Linda knew it.

At dinner, Linda drank more than a few V.O.s and water, followed by wine with dinner. Though the dinner went pleasantly enough, Laffit quietly fumed. On the way home they fought.

"You arranged this tonight."

"I did not!"

"Don't lie to me. It was supposed to be just the two of us."

"It's always just the two of us."

"What's that supposed to mean?"

The longer they fought, the more emotional each became. At one point, Linda attempted to exit the car while Laffit was driving. He reached over to slam the door shut while steering with his left hand.

By the time they arrived home the fight had escalated into a screaming match. Once inside the house, Linda declared she couldn't stay under the same roof as Laffit and stormed out. Knowing she would be a danger on the road, to herself and others, Laffit followed her out to stop her from getting behind the wheel.

Linda walked to the gate at the bottom of the driveway and had begun to open it when Laffit came from behind and grabbed her around her stomach to drag her back inside. Linda swung around and struck Laffit in the head, then grabbed on to his hair.

"Let go of my hair," Laffit instructed her. He grabbed for Linda's other arm but got hold of her pearls which broke off her neck and scattered onto the lawn. Linda continued pulling hard on his hair.

"Let go of my hair," he yelled again. When she didn't comply, Laffit grabbed for her hair and yanked a chunk out. The driveway was steep and without warning Linda suddenly slipped backwards, falling hard against the pavement.

Her fall ended the fight. When she could finally get up Laffit helped his wife into the house and put her to bed. Though she was bruised, he was grateful she was safely in bed and that the fighting was over.

It was not the evening he'd envisioned.

The following day Linda was in a great deal of pain, but nothing compared to the mental pain both were in. Neither spoke before Laffit went off to the track that morning. When he came home, he discovered Linda had been taken to Cedars-Sinai Hospital complaining of stomach pain.

When a nurse came in to examine her, she noted the bruises on Linda's arms and midriff and questioned where they had come from. Linda explained what had happened, making light of their disagreement. But the nurse seemed reluctant to accept her explanation and asked if she wanted to file charges against her husband. She quickly said no. Later, Linda told Laffit about the nurse's suspicions.

Linda was in the hospital for three days while they ran tests to find the source of her pain. The antibiotics they gave her seemed to help, but only barely.

Linda's physical state took priority over any grievance the couple had with one another. They both wanted her to feel better. When doctors couldn't find anything wrong, Laffit took Linda home to recover.

Only she didn't.

Some doctors suggested Linda was making up her symptoms, that she wanted attention, which infuriated Laffit. He knew in his heart that her pain was genuine. Linda was many things, but she was not self indulgent nor hypochondriacal.

At long last doctors determined that Linda was suffering from a burst appendix and rushed her into surgery. By then, however, days had gone by and many of Linda's organs were now dangerously affected by the gangrene that had spread, requiring extensive surgery into multiple organs.

Post surgery, Linda did not recover the way doctors expected. She was sent home but when the pain failed to subside, two more surgeries were performed to repair adhesions from the first surgery. Privately, Laffit and Linda were uncertain that doctors really knew what was causing the pain.

After the surgery Linda felt somewhat better but recovery was slow and her depression increased. Nothing anyone did or suggested seemed to help. And as hard as her family tried to cheer her up, they couldn't.

Drugs were now prescribed with increased regularity. Linda was ingesting multiple medicines and stifling her depression with alcohol. Laffit had no clue that Linda was drinking, but close friends did.

When her sister Millie, concerned over Linda's health, flew out for a visit, Linda's mood perked up. Millie even extended her visit because she was so worried about Linda's state, but eventually Millie had to go back home to New York. With her sister gone, Linda retreated into her room.

Friends Cindy Shoemaker and Roseann wondered if they should talk to Laffit about their concerns but Shoe advised them to stay out of it, it was none of their business.

Going to the track, which Linda always loved, no longer held any interest for her. Despite invitations or proddings, Linda refused everyone. She didn't want to go anywhere, see anyone, or do anything. Linda complained to Laffit that there was no fun in her life anymore. Even their sexual relationship, which had been good even in the worst of times, suddenly closed off. They were two separate human beings inhabiting the same house, but living in two different worlds.

Thirteen-year-old Lisa spent hours with her mother, chatting, watching *Days of Our Lives, The Price is Right,* and doing her teenage best to cheer her mother up. But this was a larger job than any child could possibly handle.

THE RUN
FOR THE ROSES

CHAPTER 17

The plane landed before the light of dawn touched the sky. For May it was cold, even for Kentucky, but then spring had been damper than usual, thanks to a heavy season of hurricanes. Laffit hoped the dampness in the air would not turn to rain.

He gathered his suitcase from the turnstile and headed to the cab stand. He had purposely taken the red-eye so he'd have these hours of quiet before the all-hell-breaking-loose kind of day he knew lay ahead of him. He was used to jetting to important meets and award ceremonies, but today's was the first major race at which he'd ever arrived alone. The appendectomy and all the complications that followed had sapped the vitality from his once supportive wife which meant he was traveling solo.

Luckily his current agent, Tony Matos, drove him to the airport. They ate at the steakhouse at the Marriott hotel and then Tony dropped him off at the terminal, saying he was sorry he couldn't be with him tomorrow. Stepping out of the car Laffit told him, "I think this horse is going to win and win big tomorrow." Tony grinned, hoping it was true.

Laffit's positive attitude was remarkable considering that this was his eleventh attempt. He was growing tired of reading in the papers that he'd never won. But he couldn't blame the sports writers. Sometimes he wondered himself if it would ever happen.

The previous year his horse, Caveat, came in third. Laffit had liked his chances with that horse. It had started out a beautiful day when suddenly dark clouds covered the sky and then opened up. It poured rain just as the race got underway and once on the track the mud flew up in chunks. Laffit was momentarily blinded when he went around the turn at the three-quarter pole. He had a fraction of a second to make a decision and he made the wrong one. The hole between two horses got too close and Laffit steadied the horse, which cost him the race. (Laffit's instincts about Caveat being a winner were accurate. Five weeks later he rode the horse to victory in the Belmont Stakes.)

He'd come in second on Rumbo in 1980. Between the half-mile and the three-eighths pole another jockey cracked his whip and that horse bumped Laffit's. Though Rumbo was not thrown out of position, Laffit saw his horse's ears prick. The horse sulked for a sixteenth of a mile and in the end, Genuine Risk, a filly, beat hard-charging Rumbo.

The most painful almost-win was 1973's ride on Sham. Sham was coming into the stretch, when suddenly Secretariat (who would go on to win the Triple Crown that year) came out of nowhere to overtake him. In a remarkable showing, Secretariat ran the fastest time in Kentucky Derby history. But Sham, with Laffit on board, clocked in at 1:59 4/5, the second fastest horse in Kentucky Derby history, a record that remains to this day.

Doubt *had* to be shoved out of Laffit's mind this try. Close calls, past losses, lingering doubts, all had to be ignored. He was there today to win.

Laffit had spent the last few months preparing and riding more carefully, something that went against his grain. He feared two things—being injured or being suspended. And he'd made it.

Jockey Eddie Maple who always rode for trainer Woody Stephens was given first choice between Stephens' two contenders, Devil's Bag and a horse named Swale. Devil's Bag had triumphed as a brilliant two-year-old and transitioned well into a winning three-year old. Maple took Devil's Bag, the favored horse in the race, and Laffit was given Swale. Swale was no slouch but odds were that he'd come in behind a horse named Althea.

Weeks before the Kentucky Derby, Laffit brought Swale to a triumphant victory in the Florida Derby, finishing in near record time. Then on April 28, less than ten days before the Kentucky Derby, Devil's Bag won the Derby Trial race, normally a good omen. After the race, however, x-rays revealed an ominous chip in the horse's right knee. A decision had to be made, and quickly. Did they risk running the horse in order to claim a Kentucky Derby win, or pull the horse now to protect him from possible injury? As Devil's Bag was the linchpin of a $36 million syndication, the painful decision was made to retire the horse to Claiborne Farms. It was simply too dangerous to risk losing the potential stud fees the horse would bring in. (The decision turned out to be a wise move. Devil's Bag produced progeny generating earnings of more than $47 million.)[20]

Suddenly Eddie Maple had to scramble for a Derby mount.

The man at the desk at Executive West Hotel in Louisville remembered Laffit from last year's visit and wished him luck that day. Laffit went to his room, unpacked his few items, and lay on the bed. Though he'd slept on the plane, it was not restful. He hoped he could drift off for a few hours of sleep. He phoned the desk for a 10:30 AM wake-up call, then laid his head on the pillow, willing himself to clear his mind.

The wake-up call came sooner than he'd imagined. He had fallen asleep and it took a minute to realize where he

---

[20] "Devil's Bag Euthanized Due to Broken Leg," Glenye Cain, *ESPN Horse Racing, www.ESPN.com,* February 4, 2005.

was. Laffit's nerves started jumping. This was it—again—the race of all races, the brass ring, the dream, the pinnacle, the run for the roses. He got on his knees.

"Dear Lord, I know in the past I've asked you to protect me out there. I never asked you before, but today, if you could give me just a *little* push, I'd appreciate it."

He hoped today would be the day. Swale was different; he could feel it. He'd liked the horse right from the beginning: the dark elegance, the calm composure. Being the son of Seattle Slew meant speed was inbred; the horse had talent. He also liked to come from behind, something Laffit enjoyed doing. He liked the element of surprise, the excitement of overtaking others for the win. The fact that Swale was a sibling of Landaluce only enhanced Laffit's feelings for the horse.[21]

During the Florida Derby he'd felt the steadiness of the horse, the measured speed, and the way he responded to the gentle commands Laffit imposed. He felt lucky that Eddie Maple had passed on Swale.

Trainer Woody Stephens was excited by the Florida Derby win. Odds began to rise for Swale. Two weeks before the Kentucky Derby, Woody decided to give Swale another run. He wanted to make sure he was ready so he entered him in the Lexington Stakes at Keeneland. Some trainers prefer to rest a horse before a race as big as the Derby but Stephens thought the prep race would do Swale some good.

---

[21] "Suddenly A Young Champion Is Gone," William Leggett, *Sports Illustrated*, June 25, 1984.

The race proved a disaster. Swale lost and Laffit's agent begged him to ride another horse, but Laffit refused. He had an instinct, he told Matos. "I've got faith in this horse. I know he threw a bad race today, but the track was sloppy from the rain. He's a good horse. I'm sticking with him."

Now in the hotel room, looking at the overcast sky, he hoped he wouldn't regret his decision. Horses are like people. They have good days and bad ones. He needed Swale to have a good day today.

Winning the Kentucky Derby had begun to feel elusive to Laffit. Maybe he would be like Manuela Ycaza and never win. He'd certainly never meet the records of Eddie Arcaro and Bill Hartack, both of whom had five Derby wins, that much he knew. All he needed was this one, he told himself.

In his heart he felt this was his last shot. But he couldn't go there. He had to focus on success. What he had to see in his mind was the win.

He grabbed his bag and headed to the track. When he got to Churchill Downs, the entire place felt ebullient. From the minute his cab stopped, everyone who saw him was yelling good luck. He made his way through the crowd, many of whom were begging for autographs. He signed a few and explained to people he was running late. It was 1 PM and though the big race didn't start for hours, he needed the time.

Shortly after, he entered a chaotic jocks' room. People were everywhere. Some wanted him to sign the usual: posters, photos, glasses, programs. Others wanted autographs.

The commotion was overwhelming. All he wanted to do was to focus on the race, to find a quiet corner where he could calm himself. Newsmen swooped in.

"Excuse me, Laffit, *ABC News* would like an interview."

"Laffit, can we get your photo for *Newsweek?*"

"*Sports Illustrated* has someone who'd like a quote from you."

"*The New York Times* just needs one minute of your time, Mr. Pincay," and so it went. Owners came to wish him luck, trainers came by, friends stopped in, including Ted Cliffort who wanted to wish him luck. He whispered in Laffit's ear, "No hard feelings, buddy, but I'm going to bet $100,000 on Althea to win today." Laffit shook his head and looked his friend in the eye. "Ted, it's fine if you don't want to bet on me but trust me, Althea is not going to win this race. I know that horse and she's not gonna beat Swale." Cliffort pulled back and eyed Laffit with a puzzled expression.

From the monitor in the jockeys' room Laffit could see the other races flying by. His race, the big race, was drawing near.

He went to the hotbox for a few minutes to clear his head and escape the crowd. He had to replay the race in his head and he couldn't do it in a room teeming with people.

A major concern that day was his stamina. The exertion of the first race opens a jockeys' lungs and wears him out, resulting sometimes in a jockey not having all the energy he needs to finish the race successfully. After that race the body is primed, but the first one demands all you've got. Laffit was concerned because he didn't have an earlier race that day.

In the hotbox he spent his time planning. He'd pulled post position fifteen which meant he was toward the outside. He'd have to position the horse quickly so he wouldn't lose ground on the first turn. He decided to break quickly and move the horse to the inside, but he would have to do it without running into trouble. He needed to race clean; he had to avoid trouble from others; and he had to hope that no one shut him off. After he visualized the race from start to finish in his head, he went to dress.

Laffit finished donning the Claiborne yellow silks when Seth Hancock came in to wish him luck. Laffit was happy to see Seth, but it just added to his internal pressure. He wanted to win for Seth. He was a great owner, and he deserved the win as much as anyone.

Finally, they called for the jockeys to assemble. As usual, Laffit was the last to leave the jocks' room. It was a silly ritual perhaps, done more for the silence than anything else, but today of all days, every ritual had to be followed. As per his mother's instructions, his underwear was on inside-out (keeping the luck inside.) You don't mess with success, especially today.

The first thing Laffit noticed when he got outside was the muddy earth. It had rained while he'd been in the jocks' room. He hoped Swale could make the adjustment but he wasn't sure.

On the short walk to the paddock, people waved or offered their best wishes. The paddock was crammed with people, including Swale's trainer Woody Stephens. They'd released Woody from the hospital only a half-hour before the race.[22] Woody had been battling emphysema for some time and had lost a great deal of weight. He looked frail that afternoon, but clearly Woody wanted to be there. And given his questionable physical state, Laffit wanted to make sure this Derby would be a special one for his old friend. Mike Griffit, Woody's right hand man, had taken over the training while Woody was ill. Laffit knew Mike from his days with owner Fred Hooper. He liked the man, but it was Woody he wanted to win for.

"Well, son," Woody said with a firm arm on his shoulder, "I think this horse is ready to run a big race today. Are you?"

"Yes, sir, I am."

"Then you go out there and just do your best, and I'll be happy."

It was so like Woody to believe in a man, but allow him to save face in case things didn't work out.

"Don't worry, Woody, I'll do my best."

"You always do, Laffit."

With that, Mike handed Swale off to the stable boy who walked the horse in a circle and checked the saddle. Swale looked good that day—bright, steady, with just enough edge to seem perfectly alert.

---

[22] "Swale on the Rail for the Roses," Tom Callahan, *Time Magazine*, May 14, 1984.

The call came to mount the horses and slowly they began to be led out. When the first horse entered the track, silence reigned and the opening strains of "My Old Kentucky Home" came over the loud speakers. Everyone was standing at attention—men in morning coats, women with elaborate hats on their heads. The sweet lyrics and plaintiff notes made everyone sentimental, with or without mint juleps. When the song was finished, there wasn't a dry eye in the stadium, including the jockeys'.

One by one the horses entered the track and circled round to take their places at the gate. The gate crew was efficient and the assistant starter who met Laffit firmly guided the horse into the gate.

"I want him straight. Don't let him move." Laffit told the man.

"Okay."

"He's moving his head. Don't let him. Keep him right there. I don't want him to lose his focus."

Laffit was convinced it was crucial that Swale break out of the gate fast so that he could angle him quickly toward the rail. He knew that when the bell went off, the metal of the gate would jangle and get the horse's attention. But gates open a fraction of a second before the bell sounds. If Swale didn't hear the crack of the gate and didn't move immediately, there was no way Swale would break out of the pack and it would be extremely difficult to win. With twenty horses, Laffit was going to have to work hard, and fast, to establish position. He was praying that no other horse bumped him, that he himself didn't tangle with another horse, and that Swale was up for the run of his life.

He stood poised on the horse as he watched the other jockeys move into the gate, concentrating on the strategy he had to use to maneuver to the rail.

He watched the last horse being led in and prepared for the launch. The bell went off and they flew out of the gate. Swale obeyed the commands immediately and began angling to his left. But Laffit wasn't the only jockey moving inward, he had to ride carefully to not to interfere with any other horse. The ground thundered under him, so many horses vying for the sweet spot on the rail.

By the first turn, Laffit and another jockey were both inching toward the rail, slanting like trees following the rays of the sun. Swale's head was up, his clip was good.

Four horses were in strong positions and Swale was one of them. Heading into the three-quarter pole, Althea was in the lead. Swale was known as a stalker and liked to stay purposely behind. The third and fourth horses were far enough behind, but in a race like this, any horse could emerge to challenge him.

Swale was running smoothly. His ears were up. The horse was relaxed and rating at a good pace. Laffit was biding his time, waiting for the right moment. He didn't pull back too far. Finally the time was right and Laffit passed Althea and took his place in front on the inside of the track. It was sticky underfoot so Laffit tried to correct Swale's position and place him back on the outside where the ground was firmer which would be less tiring for the horse, but the horse resisted Laffit's urgings. Swale liked where he was so Laffit opened him up there, and the horse took off like the wind.

For fifteen glorious seconds on his way to the finish line Laffit was aware that he was riding the winner of the Kentucky Derby. The seconds were lived in elongated, treasured slow motion. He was a full four lengths ahead of Althea who was now losing steam quickly. Laffit turned to be sure there was no other threat. He had nothing to worry about. Swale was widening the lead.

The announcer roared, "It's Swale all the way!"

A million thoughts competed in Laffit's mind, the largest being the realization that the eleventh time, finally, was the charm. He'd gotten his "push" and had escaped the curse. He would be able to claim the most precious prize a jockey ever wins, the Kentucky Derby.

He finished the one and a quarter mile in 2:02 2/5.

Laffit on Swale, after the Kentucky Derby win May 5, 1984

As he crossed the finish line he wished his family was there—his mother, his sister and brothers, and his son and daughter. They would be so proud. And of course, Linda, his greatest fan—the person who rooted for him more than he himself did sometimes—would be delirious.

He slowed the horse and thought back to the beginning when he feared the size of the horses he so desperately wanted to ride. He thought of the struggles with food and the personal hell he had to endure just to sit atop a horse each day and today, it was all worth it. He would be able to say, forever, that he had won the Kentucky Derby! God had listened to his prayer that morning. He was so grateful.

He stood on the horse to bring him to a slower pace but he didn't want the moment to end. He was bursting with excitement and never wanted to dismount.

The roar from the crowd took a moment to register. He'd done it! By three and a quarter lengths! He raised his arm in victory and pumped it in the air. The other riders were coming up to him. Mike Smith was the first to gallop alongside. "Congratulations!" Smith yelled, grinning ear to ear. "Welcome to the club," Bill Shoemaker shouted. Eddie Maple, who could have been on Swale and ended up in third place with At The Threshold, along with the other jockeys, sidled up, offered congratulations, genuinely pleased for him. Chris McCarron was good-natured about the loss. Althea, his horse that was leading so strongly, and was the Derby favorite, fizzled in that final stretch—as horses sometimes do—and came in nineteenth.

Laffit was touched by the jockeys' offers of congratulations. He knew what it felt like to lose. He knew the sour taste of disappointment in the back of the mouth. Losing meant you had to wish for too many things in the following year: that you'd be asked to ride in another Derby, that you'd get a horse that could win and of course, that you'd ride that race clean. And that you were still racing. Period. He'd seen many a jockey permanently sidelined not by choice, but by injury. Losing the Derby held the possibility of being your last Derby try.

A swarm of people began to circle the horse, grabbing the reins, leading him to the winner's circle. Swale was guided there by a man in a formal red jacket and black riding hat, surrounded by a mad group of people all yelling their joy and congratulations. Laffit felt as though he were floating above his horse. Ladies in their elaborate hats waved excitedly toward him. Men pumped his hand up and down, thanking him for the great ride. Ted Cliffort, who looked more excited than the owners, yelled across the crowd, "I took your advice. I bet on *you*!" Laffit was relieved and happy for his friend.

And there in the midst of the crowd stood Woody, the man he'd ridden for for many years. Suddenly he didn't look as though he'd been ill. (Woody Stephens proved stronger than many imagined. He lived another fifteen years, but this would be his last Kentucky Derby win. Later in life he would say that Swale was his all-time favorite horse.)[23] "You did well, my boy. But I knew you were gonna do it."

The traditional blanket of vibrant red roses was placed over Swale's neck. Laffit glanced down from his place in the saddle and marveled at the sight. The garland was adorned with the seal of the Commonwealth of Kentucky on one end, and the twin spires of Churchill Downs on the other. In the center of the blanket was the lone red rose pointing upward, symbolizing the struggle and the heart needed to reach the winner's circle. He would bring the single rose home to Linda. Laffit reached for it just as he was handed the winning rider's bouquet—sixty long stemmed roses.

Photographers were having a field day, lights flashing, camera's rolling. The reporters he'd met in the jockeys' room a few hours earlier were back, shoving microphones his way.

"What does it feel like to finally win the Kentucky Derby, Laffit?"

"It feels fantastic."

"How are you going to celebrate?"

"Well, I'm not celebrating tonight. I have an important race tomorrow at Hollywood Park."

"Your family must be so proud. Are they with you?"

"Unfortunately, they are back in California. My wife has been ill."

The ceremony began and the governor of Kentucky, Martha Layne Collins, spoke.

---

[23] "Woody Stephens, 84, Hall of Fame Horse Trainer, Dies," Joseph Durso, *The New York Times*, August 23, 1998.

"It is my distinct honor to present to Seth Hancock and Claiborne Farms the 1984 Kentucky Derby winner's trophy." The crowd erupted into a frenzy. Seth held the golden trophy high above his head. His wife and children were delirious with joy.

Little did the Hancocks know that this joy would be so short-lived. The following month, their beloved Swale, a mere nine days after winning the prestigious Belmont Stakes, would die from a heart attack while being given a bath, an unexpected and tragic ending for an heroic horse.

When the ceremony was over, Laffit experienced his second highlight of the day—he was introduced to Olivia Newton-John!

Laffit called home from the airport. Linda sounded tired but told her husband she was thrilled for him.

"I saw Jim McKay interview you. You did great."

"I wish you'd been here today."

"Me, too. You *won* honey, you did it! I knew you would."

"I wanted to win for you."

"It's the best medicine you could have given me."

People on the plane were generous with their praise, even thrilled to be on board with the winning jockey of the Kentucky Derby. After receiving their congratulations and signing autographs, Laffit closed his eyes and leaned back to rest. He remembered last year's flight home, after losing on Caveat.

Eddie Delahoussaye, that year's winner, and his wife Juanita had been on board. At one point Eddie graciously said to Linda. "Here, let me give you a rose from my bouquet."

Linda looked straight at Eddie and said, "No thank you. I want Laffit to give me a rose."

Eddie quietly pulled back while Laffit sat fuming.

When they got into the car, Laffit was furious. "You just made an ass of yourself on that plane. And of me, too." Linda turned and looked out the car window. They didn't speak the rest of the night, nor the next day when he left for the track.

When he got home that day Linda told him she'd called Juanita and Eddie and apologized. Laffit was surprised and pleased.

He got off the plane at LAX and not only was his agent Tony there, but his mother as well. It was midnight yet there she was, clearly excited.

"Momma, what are you doing here?"

"How could I not come and see you?"

She hugged and kissed her son.

"You made me so proud today."

"Thank you, Momma. How did you get here?"

"I took a cab."

"You took a cab at this hour of the night?

"Si, it's a special occasion." She held his cheeks between her hands. Her eyes were dancing.

"My son won the Kentucky Derby today!"

"But this is so late for you to be up. We have to get you home."

"I don't need to sleep. Laffit, I saw the race, I heard the crowd cheering you."

"You watched?" Laffit's mother never watched. She was too terrified of seeing her son injured.

"Just the end. Everyone yelled for me to come into the den, that you were going to win. So I ran in and saw you cross the finish line. It was very exciting. You deserve today. Don't you forget that."

"Thank you, Momma. Come, we'll drop you off."

"No, no, I'm in the other direction. I'll take a cab. You go straight home. I know Linda will be anxious to see you." They argued for a few minutes but Rosario wouldn't think of delaying Laffit's arrival home.

After they put his mother in a cab, Tony drove Laffit home.

Tony was as excited as Laffit about the win. "This is going to open up an exciting time for us, my friend."

"I sure hope so," replied Laffit, praying his slump was finally over.

"You are golden right now."

"Let's just hope I stay healthy."

"You will, you will."

When they got to the house, Tony gave Laffit a bear hug and congratulated him again. Laffit couldn't wait to go in and see Linda.

Linda had dreamed about a Derby win as much as Laffit had. They had talked about what it would be like, how they would feel. He couldn't wait to see her excitement and share his own.

He opened the front door. The entrance light was on but the inside of the house was dark. He tiptoed to their bedroom and quietly turned the knob. The room was also dark. There, by a faint light from the bathroom, he saw Linda, in their bed, fast asleep.

He quietly put his luggage down and slipped out of his clothes. He sat on the edge of the bed, bone weary. It had been a long, long day. He suddenly felt the deep exhaustion. He slipped under the covers and into bed and turned to his wife. She remained asleep, her chest gently rising and falling.

He placed the rose beside her.

NIGHTMARE

CHAPTER 18

In January of 1985, Laffit came home from the track one day to find Linda in an extremely affectionate mood. She hugged and kissed Laffit and laughed, something that in the old days would have been normal, but lately was out of character for Linda. Then he noticed that Linda was slurring her words. He asked if she'd been drinking, which Laffit prohibited in the house. He didn't want his children to see alcohol consumed in a casual manner. Linda's mood immediately darkened. She took offense at the accusation and fled to their bedroom.

Laffit began to clean up the den and while clearing away some glasses noticed that one still had a lot of water in it. He discovered the 'water' was actually vodka. Laffit rushed into the bedroom and confronted his wife. Linda hated lying of any sort and now Laffit had caught her in one. Linda claimed it was her sister Millie's drink, but Millie had left their home a week earlier.

Infuriated by the lie, Laffit stormed out of the bedroom.

The couple went to bed that night without speaking. The next morning, Laffit got ready to leave for the track. Linda was awake and seemingly back to normal, but he was still fuming so simply said, "I'll see you later," and left.

The family at Del Mar.

A few hours later, Laffit got a frantic phone call from thirteen-year-old Lisa. Laffit heard:

"Daddy, I had to call the paramedics for Mommy."

And with that, they were into the abyss.

Of course there were signs. Those who knew Linda had been concerned. Cindy Shoemaker had spoken with Roseann about it often. They worried Linda was in serious trouble—but ultimately felt they might be over-stepping their bounds if they said anything to Laffit. Besides, he lived with Linda. Who would know better than he that his wife was in desperate shape?

Lately Linda made up excuses not to have lunch with Roseann, or go shopping, or grab dinner, or see a movie, or take the kids for an outing, or any of the fun things they used to do regularly. She became reclusive.

Roseann also noticed that Linda had begun drinking vodka early in the day. When she commented to Linda that she needed to slow down on the drinking, Linda responded, "Do you think I *like* having to drink?"

But the girls—Linda, Roseann and Cindy—were making plans for that Sunday. They were all going to Chasen's together to watch the Super Bowl game. Roseann was bolstered by discussions about who was wearing what, and how they were going to do their hair. It felt normal, so she lowered the red flag waving in her brain.

It was only in hindsight that people recognized what had been happening.

The month previous, Linda had insisted on throwing a big bash to celebrate Laffit's birthday.

"I don't need a party. You're not feeling that well. I don't want you to go to all that trouble," Laffit argued.

"But I want to. It will be fun. You know how I love to plan these kinds of things."

"Why don't you wait until it's my fortieth?

"I don't want to wait."

It was an event Laffit did not want, even begged her not to do, especially in her weakened state. But Linda wanted the party as a way to reintroduce herself to everyone after her long illness, to be seen as Mrs. Laffit Pincay again, to prove she was well. She tented the backyard, hired a band, arranged for a caterer (Matteo's) and chose a florist. Hundreds of their nearest and dearest were invited.

Unfortunately, the day of the party, unhappy news was delivered. Though Laffit had won racing's money title that year, that afternoon Laffit was told that the Eclipse Award, which everyone just assumed was his, was in fact, not. It would go to his friend Angel Cordero. Laffit had worked hard all year. He'd even won the Kentucky Derby. Though he'd hoped to win the Eclipse Award, he hadn't counted on it. Linda, however, was devastated. The news arriving on the day of the party put her into a spin.

She frantically placed a call to Roseann. "Can you come early?" Naturally, Roseann rushed right over. Millie, Lisa and Young Laffit were also there bolstering Linda as best they could. When the time for the party came, her sister Millie had to coax Linda out of the bedroom because suddenly Linda was nervous." Go have a good time!" Millie exclaimed, then led her sister out to greet the people who had begun to arrive.

A line of limousines snaked their way up Cummings Drive. Laffit, though initially uncertain about the party, greeted friends warmly and played the perfect host. Linda, now relaxed, floated around the room making sure guests had anything and everything they needed.

"Vince, so glad you could make it. You're looking as handsome as ever," Linda said as she patted DeGregory's arm. Vince was delighted to find Linda so warm, so friendly.

Linda looked radiant that night in an emerald green satin skirt with a sequined sweater to match. Her luxurious honey colored hair glimmered. She sported new earrings (a Christmas gift from Laffit) and wore her favorite diamond necklace from him. It was hard to believe she'd ever been ill. She positively glowed.

Linda and Laffit the night of the big party.

At one point in the evening she pulled Humberto into a corner. Humberto, one of Laffit's oldest friends, was part of the Panamanian contingency Laffit enjoyed spending evenings with. After they sat, Linda took Humberto's hands and looked deeply in his eyes, "Listen, Humberto I just wanted to take a moment to thank you for being such a great friend to Laffit all these years. I know you really care about him and I appreciate that. He trusts you and I can see why." It was such an unusual occurrence, that Humberto told Laffit about it the next day.

A month later people would look back on the evening and shake their heads. How could they have been so blind?

Roseann came early and stayed late. That night, Linda hadn't wanted anyone to leave. She begged people to stay. Roseann treasures a small Polaroid photo that Young Laffit took that night of she and Linda sitting on a couch. It's the last picture they ever took together.

Roseann and Linda that night, the last photo Roseann had taken with her friend.

To this day, everyone wonders what they could have done to save Linda. "Maybe I should have called Marge Everett.

She had some real influence." Roseann says. But Marge had arranged for the psychiatrist that visited Linda in the hospital after her third attempt—the doctor Linda dismissed. Cindy says she too still harbors guilt that she couldn't help her friend.

But could anyone have done anything? When you're asking the question about someone you deeply love, someone who was in serious trouble and you knew it, and someone who consistently refused to get help no matter how hard you pleaded, the question is a haunting one. Yet to this day— over twenty years later—it weighs upon the people who loved Linda, and feel they failed her.

Such is the painful legacy of suicide.

Lisa, Linda's daughter, was perhaps the most perceptive about her mother's state, at least on a subliminal level. But she was only fifteen-years-old at the time and far too young to grasp the enormity of the signs around her.

Certainly during the weeks leading up to the suicide, she'd witnessed some significant changes in her mother's behavior. Linda began slurring her words. When Lisa asked why, Linda told her she thought it was flashbacks from all the anesthesia she'd had during her surgeries. Her mother was driving one day and continually tapped other car's bumpers but dismissed it when Lisa expressed concern. Another time Linda told Lisa she thought their phone was being tapped. Then one day she came home from school and discovered her mother had bitten her perfectly manicured fingernails down to the quick. And one night, Lisa watched her mother frantically exercising in front of the hallway mirrors until her father came out of their bedroom and gently led her back to bed. All these incidents were peculiar but no one knew they were significant.

The day it happened, Lisa had an oral presentation due in speech class. The assignment was to write something that would emotionally move the class. Lisa's choice? A suicide note.

Earlier that afternoon, at school, Lisa was summoned to the office. When she got there she was told to call her mother immediately.

"Hi, Mom. Is everything okay?"

"Oh, sweetheart, I just wanted to apologize to you for how I've been behaving lately. I'm so sorry. You know I love you, don't you?"

"I know you do, Mom, and I love you, too." Lisa was perplexed by her mother's call but was used to unusual behavior of late.

When Lisa got home, rather than find her mother curled up in bed as she normally was these days, her mother's hair was coiffed, her makeup was perfectly done and Linda was seated in the living room painting her nails. Lisa asked if she was going anywhere. "No, I just want to make up to you for being so out of it lately."

Young Laffit had brought a friend, Ian, home with him that day. The two boys went straight to Young Laffit's room to play with his gigantic Tonka trucks which the boys loved to crash into one another. Lisa went to her room to call a girlfriend. After a few minutes she heard her mother go into her room and close the door. Normally her mother didn't keep the door closed.

A short while later, Lisa heard Young Laffit skip down the hallway to his mother's room. When he got there he tried to open her door.

"Mom, open up."

"Go away, Laffit."

"I need to ask you something.

"I said, go away."

"Mom, why is the door locked?" Young Laffit pounded on the door.

"Go back to your room right now." Her voice was firm this time.

Lisa came out of her room. "What's going on?"

"Mom won't open the door."

"Go to your room, Laffit. I'll try."

Young Laffit slinked away.

Lisa knocked on the door. "Mom, it's me. Open up."

"Just go away and leave me alone."

There was a key to get into her parent's bedroom which Linda had hidden away on the top ledge of an adjoining closet. Lisa knew where it was and spent almost ten minutes looking for it. All the while she heard her mother stumbling in the bedroom.

Then she heard it. A loud pop. Something registered in her brain, though at the time, she didn't know what it was. Lisa began pounding heavily on the door.

"Mom, open the door *right now!*"

There was only silence. "Mom, answer me!"

Panic began to rise like bile in Lisa's throat. With all the strength she could muster, she raised both fists and with a swift thrust, Lisa, a fifteen-year-old, four-foot, nine-inch, one-hundred-pound girl, took the door off its hinges.

What she saw when she looked in was her mother lying on the floor, a gun in her hand, looking peaceful and beautiful.

Lisa immediately ran to her room and called 911 then went to tell Luz Maria what had happened. Luz Maria was terrified, much too terrified to go to Linda's room, so Lisa went in to check on her mother again and then she called her father.

"Daddy, I had to call the paramedics for Mommy. She shot herself."

Humberto heard his name paged at Santa Anita racetrack. He was told to go to the jockeys' room immediately. On his way there he saw Laffit racing toward him, tears running down his checks.

"You have to drive me home. It's Linda."

"What happened?"

"She's done it again."

The two men tore out of the park at ninety miles per hour.

"Can't you go any faster?" Laffit demanded.

Humberto said nothing. After a moment Laffit spoke up.

"I can't take this anymore."

"She has an illness, Laffit."

"She's driving me crazy. Look what she's putting the children through. They were home when she tried it this time."

Humberto Aguilera.

"I'm sure she doesn't mean to do these things."

"Well, enough is enough. For sure I'm getting a divorce. It's too much."

Back at the track, Bill Shoemaker called Cindy. "Something's wrong. Laffit and Humberto just flew out of here and both of them were crying."

Cindy called the Pincay home. Lisa answered. "No, everything's fine," Lisa told her. Lisa was reluctant to share the news with Cindy before she'd talked to her father. "My dad just arrived home," she told her mom's friend, "I have to hang up."

They pulled near the house and five squad cars, all with lights flashing, were parked in the driveway. When Humberto spotted them, he stopped the car.

"Laffit, you'd better get yourself ready. This doesn't look good," he whispered to Laffit.

They pulled in the driveway and the men got out of their car. Two policemen headed to them.

"Which one of you gentlemen is Mr. Pincay?"

"I am," Laffit said.

"We've taken your wife to the hospital, sir."

"Are they pumping her stomach?" Laffit asked.

The policeman turned to look at the other cop.

"Do you know what happened?"

Somehow Laffit had only heard the first half of what Lisa had told him on the phone. His mind had successfully blocked the information about Linda shooting herself.

"Not really."

"I'm afraid your wife shot herself in the head."

Laffit sank to his knees. Humberto held on to him.

"What hospital is she at?" Humberto asked.

"Hollywood Presbyterian."

Humberto whispered to Laffit, "Come, I'll take you to see her."

"The children," Laffit whispered, "First I have to see the children."

After he'd hugged both of his stunned children, they headed for the hospital.

"You can follow me," the policeman told Humberto.

At the emergency room, a doctor came out and briefly explained that the bullet had not exited Linda's head, which meant the damage was severe.

"I can assure you that everyone in the emergency room has been working very hard to help your wife."

"Thank you," was all he could utter.

On the way to the hospital he had clung to the hope that the injury was merely a graze. He couldn't believe that Linda, the woman who hated guns more than anyone, had actually used one, let alone on herself. And to the head!

"Unfortunately, we had to put your wife on a respirator."

"What does that mean?"

"Technically it means that machines are keeping her alive right now."

Laffit kept looking at the doctor, trying to take in the words he'd just spoken. When they did sink in, he began to cry.

"Please," he said, "You must do something. Bring in a specialist. I'll pay for anything, anything at all. I can't lose her. We have children."

"I don't want to offer you any false hope, Mr. Pincay. The tests are pretty conclusive, but I will admit I'm not the best neurologist in the world. That man is a doctor in Houston. I could consult with him if you want."

"Please, please call him. Bring him here. I'll get a private jet to fly him in."

When Laffit had seen Linda, had kissed her swollen, gauzed head with the trickle of blood seeping out from beneath the bandage; when he'd told her he loved her; and when all the doctors convinced him that there was nothing more that he could do right now, that she would not be waking up, he went home to his children.

Meanwhile, minutes after her father left for the hospital, Lisa called Cindy and told her what had happened. Cindy raced over to be with her friend's children. By the time Laffit returned, Luz Maria and Cindy had done their best to clean the bedroom of the stains. Cindy also called everyone, including Linda's sister Millie, to tell her the devastating news.

The house filled with people the moment they heard. All were well meaning, but the sight of them when Laffit returned was overwhelming. Laffit remembers a sea of faces. Friends hugged him tightly and told him to be strong, that they were praying things would be alright.

Then the front door flew open and Roseann came flying through the doors as wild as a tornado.

"What were you thinking?" she demanded of Laffit.

She approached him and slid to her knees sobbing.

"Why? Why? Why did you have a gun in the house?" she asked through sobs.

Laffit began to cry, too. "I never thought she'd do anything like this. Never."

The room was silent watching two people in extraordinary pain desperately trying to find reason behind madness. But there was none to find.

Everyone knew Laffit kept guns in the house for protection purposes. And everyone knew Linda was terrified of them. After three pill overdoses, Laffit never considered a gun a weapon Linda would ever use. It didn't fit with what he knew about her. She was so terrified of guns she wouldn't even allow Laffit to buy their son a toy version of one. The two real guns he had for protection were under lock and key. He didn't think Linda even knew where the keys were.

Her sister Millie knew about the gun that was kept under the bed, locked in a case. Linda was so fearful she would somehow come in contact with the gun, she was afraid of making the bed.

Laffit's mind churned over the notion that Linda had actually used a gun on herself. More disturbing was the discovery of an anatomy book in their bedroom. Since neither was interested in the subject he could only surmise that she had been studying the diagrams to determine the most effective place to aim.

More than anything, Laffit was devastated that she was so unhappy she would try something like this. The other attempts, with pills, were nowhere near as frightening. And to do it in the house when her children and Young Laffit's friend were home! Clearly, her thinking—her emotional state—was far more distorted than he'd realized.

The doctor from Houston came the next day, read the reports, repeated some tests, then ordered a few new ones. The following day he and the neurologist met with Laffit. The neurologist spoke first.

"Mr. Pincay, we have consulted for the past two days on your wife's condition."

"I hope you have some good news," Laffit said hopefully.

The Houston doctor spoke up.

"I wish we did, Mr. Pincay. Cases like this are always so tragic. We re-ran several of the tests, but the results were the same. There are no active brain-waves."

"So my wife is brain-dead?"

Both doctors were silent for a moment. "I'm afraid so," the neurologist said.

This time Laffit didn't cry.

"We know this is a hard decision but we think it best if the machines were turned off and your wife was allowed to slip away."

There was a long silence as Laffit considered what they were saying.

Friends had suggested it might come to this but Laffit had shut them off.

We have to be positive. We have to hope the doctor from Texas can help.

Laffit hadn't allowed himself to consider any other possibility.

"You're absolutely sure?" he asked the doctor.

"The tests are very clear. I'm sorry."

Laffit cleared his throat.

Linda and he had talked about this once. He knew her wishes. "I know she wouldn't want to be kept alive like this."

"It's best to remember your wife the way she was."

Laffit did not resist. He had no will of his own. He was in deep shock, and was easily led that afternoon to what the doctors suggested. He'd fought reality for three days. He couldn't fight it any longer. He agreed to allow them to turn off the machines and end Linda's life. But first he wanted to see his wife one last time.

He went alone into the dimly lit room where Linda lay. The whooshing machines pulsated. He approached his wife and saw a woman who was barely recognizable. Her head was misshapen from the bandages and the tubes coming out of her nose and mouth. The pain and fear in his heart made Laffit feel he would either burst apart or faint. He wasn't sure which.

He kissed the small part of her cheek that was exposed and gently took her hand. First he cried, then apologized for everything he'd ever done to hurt her, then he told her how sorry he was that she'd been so unhappy, and how he wished with all his heart that he'd not failed her.

When he could bear it no longer, he kissed her on the lips for the last time, whispered that he would love her forever, and left.

AFTERMATH

CHAPTER 19

The days that followed were filled with a blur of people and punishing non-stop regrets. Why hadn't he seen it coming? How could he not have known? Why had he confronted her about the vodka? Had that been the thing that put her over the edge? Why didn't he say more to her that morning before he left? Why? Why? Why? Endless questions tormented him and no answers were forthcoming.

Linda always said she would die young. Was it a self-fulfilling prophecy, he wondered, or did she have a premonition?

At the funeral, many people commented on the party she'd thrown for him. "It was almost like a farewell party," more than one friend commented. Was she planning this a month ago? Is that why she was so intent on having the party?

Linda and Laffit, reminiscent of the wedding photo.

The event that Laffit resisted, which occurred less than three weeks earlier, was now a bittersweet memory brought to life every time he saw the pictures. In one, Linda is kissing Laffit much like the wedding photo of the two of them. She seemed bright and happy in the pictures ... the way she used to be.

So much went through Laffit's mind. What should he have done differently? Why did he listen to her when she said she didn't need help? All those times when she refused help, should he have forced her? Could he have?

And now, what should he do to help his kids? How would his children ever recover? How would *he* ever recover? Endless questions played in a loop in his mind. There were no answers.

He berated himself for the moments he'd squandered. Some nights they would get into bed and she would want to talk. "I've told you over and over, Linda, don't try to talk to me when I'm going to bed. Talk to me when I get home from the track or when we're having dinner. I'm too tired now. I need my rest." Why didn't he take the time and let her talk, he asked himself over and over.

His emotional extremes were tremendous. He fluctuated between guilt over having failed her, to fury over her doing this to the three of them, to an odd kind of admiration of her strength to have done such a thing to relieve her pain. But always it ended in unrelenting grief. He couldn't believe he'd never hold her again, never hear her laugh, never smell her unique fragrance.

When Laffit returned from the hospital the day of the shooting, Lisa told him more about what had happened that day. She explained about the call her mother made to school asking Lisa's forgiveness. She told her dad about her mother's upbeat mood, her full make-up and her painted nails. The children were too young to remember their mother's earlier attempts but Laffit knew the suicide was now a permanent scar for both of them. He could not believe the horrible nightmare he was living, and that his children were being put through.

On the Monday that Linda died, *The Los Angeles Times* printed an article that caused additional agony for the family. Reporter Bill Christine not only reported that Laffit and Linda were estranged (a complete falsehood) but that Lisa and her mother had argued that afternoon and that her mother had then locked herself in her bedroom and shot herself.[24]

Seeing Lisa maligned was more than he could bear. Laffit, furious, called the reporter. After Laffit said his peace, Lisa got on the phone and said, " I don't know how this time could be any worse than it is, but you made it worse. I hope my dad sues your ass!"

The funeral was excruciating. Everyone was exceedingly kind, which in its own way was painful—to be the recipient of so much generosity. Linda's brother Ronnie was spotted sitting on a curb outside the church, drunk. He never made it inside. A mother and two sisters all dead from suicide was clearly too much for him.

Thankfully Lisa, mature beyond her years, took charge of the funeral, helped by Millie and Roseann. Marge Everett was, as always, generous with her assistance. Somehow they all got through it.

---

[24] "Linda Pincay, Wife of Jockey, Dies of Wound," Bill Christine, *The Los Angeles Times*, January 21, 1985.

When the funeral was over, a quiet descended upon the house—a quiet they both craved and feared. For the first few nights, Laffit slept in Young Laffit's room. He wasn't afraid to go to his bedroom; he just wasn't ready to feel the emptiness.

Luz Maria had finished cleaning up their bedroom and somehow made it presentable again. She brought Laffit seventeen bottles of pills she'd found in the room. They'd all been kept in a purple Crown Royal bottle bag. Laffit was stunned by the range of pills and to discover that two doctors were prescribing Valium to Linda.

Around the fourth night Laffit entered the bedroom and slept in their bed. Surprisingly, the bedroom calmed him. It was their room, a place where they had fought on occasion but also a place where they had laughed, cried, made love and made up. He felt Linda's presence in the room and it comforted him.

The following week friends and family came by and advised Laffit to go back to riding. What good did it do to sit around and mourn, more than one person pointed out.

The children wanted him to go back also. Laffit, however, just wanted to quit. He didn't have the heart to ride. But he still had a family to care for, friends argued, and he had to support them somehow. What choice did he have? What else could he do?

Three weeks after the largest emotional trauma of his life, Laffit went back to Santa Anita to ride.

Driving to the track Laffit wasn't sure he could go through with it. Walking into the jockeys' room proved more painful then he'd anticipated. Everyone was so sincere in their offerings of condolences, he didn't know if he could bear to look in anyone's eyes. Finally he entered the paddock and mounted his horse.

The entire time, Laffit had to force himself to stay aboard. He wanted desperately to jump off and leave the track altogether. As the horse broke into the sunshine and stepped onto the track, Laffit kept his eyes on the San Gabriel Mountains, a sight he and Linda both loved. What Laffit didn't notice was the crowd in the stands, rising to acknowledge his presence and gently applauding his return.

When he realized what was happening, he kept his head to his chest. He didn't want anyone to see the tears in his eyes.

He was led to the gate where thankfully routine and instinct kicked in. Laffit's focus came back and he let the horse know he was there and in charge. The horse's response was reassuring.

Once the gate was opened, Laffit's mind cleared. The one place on earth where he felt whole and apart from the rest of the world, was on the track. For two and a half minutes, his heart felt no pain.

Shortly thereafter Laffit rode Adored for old friend, trainer Laz Barrera, in the Santa Maria Handicap. Adored, Linda's favorite horse, was that day's winner, and after he crossed the finish line and the floodgates opened for Laffit. Tears he did not want fans to see came pouring out. Barrera and the children met him

Johnny Longden, Laffit, Young Laffit, Lisa Barrera and Lisa.

at the winner's circle—the place where Linda, until her illness, always joined him—but this time it was Barrera who was hugging Laffit. Laffit fell into his arms sobbing.

It was a tough return, but return he had. He knew his friends were right; he couldn't sit around the house all day mourning Linda's death.

Santa Maria Handicap. Laffit being hugged by Laz Barrera after winning on Adored.

That night at the dinner table Laffit told the children, "We miss your mother very much, and we're all feeling really sad but we have to move on, as hard as that is. Even though we know she loved us, your mother decided to leave us. So we're going to honor her and do her proud and move forward." It was a difficult thing to articulate but Laffit felt it was important to free the children from any sense of responsibility for what their mother had done. He said it as much for himself as for them. After a week, the children returned to school.

Linda's sister Millie felt it incumbent upon herself to provide some of the mothering Lisa and Young Laffit had lost. Though Millie was living in New York at the time and couldn't always physically be there, she was on the phone to the children constantly.

Roseann rushed in to help as well. Linda had been her very best friend and Roseann was devoted to her children. When Linda had told her, "They'd all be better off without me," she protested, knowing it wasn't true. Now she was seeing how right she was and how wrong Linda had been. The children, though brave, were devastated.

After each suicide attempt Linda had sworn on her children's heads that she would never do it again, that life was too precious, that she would never put them through that kind of pain she herself had experienced. She made three attempts, and tragically on the fourth try, succeeded.

Laffit's mother Rosario moved in and did the day-to-day things for the children: she got them ready for school, prepared their dinners, oversaw homework, and tucked them in bed if Laffit came home late.

The house felt hollow in the weeks that followed. The children and Laffit quickly tired of sympathetic treatment. It was not that it wasn't appreciated, but it was awkward being singled out and pitied. Teachers at school, neighbors, family, and friends were overly solicitous. The children wanted life to return to normal, or at least the new normal they were each left with. Even their young friends seemed at a loss as to how to treat them.

Each of them needed as much normalcy as they could find in life, especially during those first months. Dad being back at the track was normal. Lisa and Young Laffit going to school was normal. Trips to the grocery store, dentist appointments, and sleepovers with friends were all normal.

The family settled into this new normalcy. In fact, things were turning normal a bit too soon for Rosario's taste. After a few months Laffit couldn't stand the loneliness and began to date, much to Rosario's chagrin.

Rosario was protective of the children. It was too early, she said, for their father to be dating. And she was worried about her son. She'd witnessed his utter devastation at Linda's death. What on earth could he be thinking seeing women so soon? He needed time to heal, to recover, she believed.

But Laffit saw things differently. He was by no means ready to fall in love, but he and Linda had led a very social life, up until her illness. Suddenly being home every night felt constricting. And dangerous. He couldn't sit around and think all the time, it was driving him crazy.

Rosario refused to support Laffit's decision to date and left the house. Though he hadn't wanted his mother to leave, in some ways it forced Laffit to finally assume the role of single parent. It was time, he knew, to figure out what his life was going to be without Linda. Being just the three of them was painful but necessary.

They would go on.

Back in the Saddle

Chapter 20

Despite his personal pain, Laffit continued to ride well. As Tony Matos had predicted after his Kentucky Derby win, his professional slump came to an end. That following year, 1985, mere months after Linda died, Laffit came in second place at the Kentucky Derby on a horse called Stephan's Odyssey. He finished five lengths behind his good friend Angel Cordero on Spend A Buck.[25] With the win, Spend A Buck was automatically entered into

---

[25] "Spend a Buck, Make a Buck," Tom Callahan, *Time Magazine*, May 13, 1985.

a bonus race—that is, if the owners were willing to forego the Preakness in favor of the Jersey Derby.

Bonus races are the brass ring of racing. They're the secret wish every jockey makes when blowing out the candles on the birthday cake they never eat. Bonus races are, in short, BIG money. They come along very rarely.

This particular bonus race was created when Garden State Park owner Robert Brennan declared that if the horse that won the Kentucky Derby could go on to win the two prep races in New Jersey (the Garden State Park and the Cherry Hill Mile) and then win the Jersey Derby, he would put up a $2 million bonus. That coupled with the $600,000 Jersey Derby purse made it the richest race that had ever been run.

After the Kentucky Derby, all eyes were on Spend A Buck. But would his owners bypass the Preakness, and thereby the Triple Crown, for a chance at the money? Since the Jersey Derby was set for nine days after the Preakness there was no way the horse could keep both appointments. Owner Dennis Diaz settled the matter when he declared, "We're in the business to win purses,"[26] and the race was on.

The question remained, could Spend A Buck go on to win the two New Jersey races? With Angel Cordero at the reins, that's exactly what he did.

Spend a Buck was on a roll; he captured three out of the four races. There was only one left to go, the Garden State race. The problem was that Angel Cordero was committed

---

[26] Ibid.

to ride another horse, Track Baron, on the same day, at the same time, at Aquaduct and the trainer wouldn't let him off the hook. Cordero did everything in his power to have the Aquaduct race time moved. He even checked on having a private helicopter fly him from one track to the other. The Jersey track would not budge on the time either. Finally Cordero pleaded with the horse owner at Aquaduct but the man said "No, you're committed." The $2 million purse was so close within his grasp ... and yet so far.

When all avenues failed, the reality was that another rider had to be chosen. That rider was Laffit.

Laffit was so excited by the possibility of the race that he flew from California to New Jersey just for a day to work the horse, to get to know him better. When he rode that day, his enthusiasm soared. The horse had speed, and a gorgeous stride, well beyond what Laffit had imagined. Spend A Buck, however, was a bleeder, the only thing that worried Laffit. If the horse bled during the race, all his dreams would disintegrate.

The day of the race was filled with the extra pressures that come with high stakes races: more press, more people, and more tension. Riding a horse that is considered a cinch to win put Laffit under additional pressure. All he could do was what he always did: stay focused.

Then the gates flung open and the race was on.

Laffit had a suspicion that Huddle Up had been put in this race to press his horse. The result was a speed duel meant to tire Spend a Buck but Spend a Buck kept apace.

The horse was doing well, easily the leader in the race, until midway through when Laffit suddenly felt the horse deflate, lose his punch, simply go weak beneath him.

Laffit didn't know what was happening. He pulled out his whip and hit the horse once to get his mind back on the race. At that moment, Crème Fraiche came up to challenge Spend A Buck. Laffit rode hard to keep his horse focused and kept a tight rein. The horse responded, though not as well as Laffit had hoped. Though the horse was in the lead (barely), Laffit feared he was in physical trouble. Crème Fraiche was neck and neck with Spend A Buck.

Suddenly El Basco pushed forward. Laffit knew now that the win was impossible, the horse just didn't have it in him. Nonetheless, he rode his best, never looking back to see who was gaining, certain the others were preparing to make strong finishes and pass him by—which would happen momentarily. Laffit had been concentrating so hard on propelling the horse forward that before he realized what was happening, he'd crossed the finish line. The crowd in the stands went wild. Laffit was dazed. He couldn't believe he'd done it, that Spend A Buck had done it. He knew the horse had won on sheer courage. More than excitement, he felt relief … and exhaustion. Both he and the horse had exerted every ounce of strength and every bit of skill on this race.

The $2.6 million dollar prize certainly made up for the effort, but there was no one to share it with.

PHYLLIS

CHAPTER 21

For Laffit, though his riding was strong, his emotional recovery from Linda's death was delicate and complicated and slow. Guilt was fused with anger. But life—as it always does—triumphed. Each emotion was initially unbearable. And each one had to be given time to run its course.

Though his mother didn't understand, friends saw that Laffit was lonely, very lonely, and began introducing him to eligible women.

At the track one day, producer Aaron Spelling's wife Candy introduced Laffit to an attractive blond who managed to get Laffit to laugh—something he hadn't done in months. The attraction was immediate. The woman was ultra feminine, and was clearly interested in Laffit. Though five years older than Laffit, they began a relationship.

The woman turned out to be actress Phyllis Davis, one of the stars of the television show *Vega$* with Robert Urich. Curiously, Davis was the person who, through her sister Millie, had gotten Linda in to see psychic Peter Herkos.

Laffit, D. Wayne Lucas and Phyllis Davis

What began as a gentle flirtation quickly turned serious. Whether it was because Laffit was overwhelmingly lonely, or Phyllis overwhelmingly needy, the two soon moved in together. It was not a smart move, Laffit later observed.

At first, the children were happy to have Phyllis around. She was fun and it was good to see their father smile. Unfortunately though, the good times didn't last. Phyllis resented any signs of Linda's presence in the family home and worked swiftly to remove them. Family photos were boxed away, furniture was shifted, décor was altered. Even Millie, who knew Phyllis, was struck by her complete sanitizing of the house. Hearing that she was disposing of her sister's things, Millie asked if she could have a few of Linda's personal items. Phyllis sent her Linda's bras.

Perhaps most wrenching of all, Phyllis fired their beloved housekeeper, Luz Maria, which devastated the children. Luz Maria's departure meant the door was now open for Phyllis to have free reign. From then on she dominated the children's lives in a very unpleasant way.

Though loving, flirtatious and sexy in Laffit's presence, Phyllis grew cold when alone with the children. Both were ordered to clean and scrub and obey rules they felt were punitive. When they mentioned this to their father, he demurred to Phyllis feeling the children were exaggerating or perhaps even a bit jealous. Resentments began to build.

Phyllis, Lisa, Young Laffit, Laffit and Fred Hooper
in Miami for Eclipse Awards.

When it came to Young Laffit, both children agree that Phyllis seemed to take special glee out of making his life miserable. Phyllis, it seemed, did not have a maternal bone in her body, and seemingly little understanding of what a devastating loss the two children had recently suffered.

Young Laffit, after attending summer camp on the grounds of a military school, begged to be sent there—anything to get out of the house. Lisa was accepted at USC, but when she failed to bring home a 4.0 average on her first report card, Phyllis convinced Laffit that his hard-earned money was being wasted on her education. Lisa, under pressure, dropped out of school.

As a couple, things were going well. In private, Phyllis treated Laffit like a king. It was only when the children entered the picture that things grew difficult. That meant the children were miserable most of the time.

Phyllis involved herself in all aspects of Laffit's life and often voiced her concern to Laffit that his money was not being properly managed. Laffit grew irritated at her insinuation and broke off further discussions.

Laffit with Marge Everett.

"You've been with this accountant for twenty years. You should be making more money with your investments," Phyllis told him.

"I told you, I don't want to talk about it.

In frustration, Phyllis phoned Laffit's old friend Marge Everett to elicit help. In Marge, Phyllis found a sympathetic ear. Marge called and asked Laffit to get her a list of all his investments and because it was Marge asking and not Phyllis, he did. His manager was not happy with the request but turned over the list.

A few days later Marge contacted Laffit. "I'm afraid I have some very disturbing news," she warned. His investments were virtually worthless.

Vincent Andrews, Jr., Laffit's money manager, was not some fly-by-night character Laffit had found on his own. Laffit's years of hob-knobbing had put him in elite circles where he met Vincent Sr., a man who came with impeccable credentials. The two clicked immediately and Laffit was delighted to have someone who understood what it was he wanted done with his money. When the senior Andrews died, his son took over his business and Laffit—and his investments—stayed put. Laffit and Andrews, Jr. began doing business together in the 1970s when Laffit was doing extraordinarily well financially.

Andrews paid the bills and had put Linda and Laffit on an allowance of $250 a week. The couple thought they were being smart and thrifty.

Jockeying is a precarious trade that can end any minute. One injury can destroy years of dedication and success. Any smart jockey knows he must save for the future as jockeys do not have the luxury of pensions. Laffit wanted someone who was conservative enough to protect his nest egg but clever enough to latch on to deals that would increase his holdings.

Laffit's understanding was that Vince, Jr. was investing his earnings in a variety of ways. What Laffit did not know was that on top of the five percent per year that Laffit was giving Andrews to manage his money, the man was also making ten percent for every investment he put Laffit into. Many of those investments turned out to be with Andrew's friends. Any investments that Laffit brought his way via people he met were all rejected— undoubtedly because they wouldn't have netted Andrews his lucrative ten percent.

One investment involved a house in Del Mar that a man was selling for far below market value. Laffit wanted the house badly but Andrews nixed the idea. To this day, Laffit is still frustrated that he passed on a beach house that's now worth many millions.

Andrews' investments, though not illegal, were nonetheless far too speculative for a client who required financial security. Laffit had been told about hotels and limited partnerships he was buying into. What he got in actuality were highly speculative financial disasters. For Laffit, the greatest career earning jockey of all time, to not be on financial bedrock seemed ludicrous, if not criminal. Laffit, it turned out, was on quicksand.

The news was a huge blow to Laffit. He was barely recovered from the loss of Linda and now all his assets, almost $5 million in total, were virtually gone. Marge quickly suggested another accounting firm, (ironically Arthur Anderson LLP, who later lost their license due to their involvement with Enron.) The people at Anderson found that Andrews not only made bad investments, he made serious errors on Laffit's taxes. Laffit owed $300,000 in back taxes and was informed he had exactly three days to come up with the money.

Laffit sued Andrews but the man immediately filed for bankruptcy. Andrews claimed he was broke—yet managed to keep working and paying his attorney.

As it turned out, Phyllis' instincts were extremely helpful.

At home Laffit could not enjoy a peaceful environment. Young Laffit was off to military school and Lisa left to go live with her grandmother. Still Phyllis became more demanding.

Laffit wondered how he'd gotten himself into this mess, then remembered and missed Linda all over again.

Through it all, he raced. In 1987, Laffit accomplished something no other jockey had ever done. He won seven races in a day at Santa Anita Racetrack. It was March 14. Laffit had not ridden in the first race. After bringing in Polly's Ruler and Texas Wild and then Cracksman to first place in the second, third and fourth race, a buzz began in the stands. Fairways Girl in the fifth race and Looking-forthebigone in the sixth raised excitement to a fever pitch. The fact that everyone was betting on Laffit, and thereby lowering the odds, didn't matter one whit. People were watching history unfold and they knew it. A few jockeys had won five races in a day, but six was near to impossible and seven was unheard of.

Laffit wins seven races in one day, May 14, 1987

The day had not started out with promise. The night before Laffit had dinner with Phyllis at El Cache, a restaurant near their home. Laffit's sister Margie and her husband were back from a few months visit in Panama. Joining them that night was Laffit's mother. Since Rosario had moved out of Laffit's home after Linda's death, the two had been at odds. For months they had not spoken. This night would be a reconciliation and everyone was on their best behavior. It was not that Laffit didn't love his mother, he just didn't like her insinuating herself into his personal life. That night, they forgave the differences. Laffit ate more than normal and even had some wine. The next morning he arrived at the track in less than stellar condition.

Luckily one of the valets had a neck massager that Laffit used for fifteen minutes which revived him—enough to go out and win five raccs in a row. Could he capture even more that day?

In the jocks' room, fellow jockeys began gathering around the monitor, rooting Laffit along. For the seventh race he was aboard Integra and sailed to the finish line. The crowd went wild.

In the stands, everyone was up, eagerly anticipating the eighth race. For that race, Laffit had a choice between two horses. One he had ridden the previous week and won on, but instead he chose to ride Bob Back. He felt confident in that race and was floating easily into the home stretch when out of nowhere came Bill Shoemaker who beat him.

For the ninth race—Laffit's try for the seventh win—Laffit was on Bedouin. Of all the days, of all the races, he couldn't believe his bad luck. Bedouin was one of those horses that liked to race, but didn't like to win. All Laffit could think as he was changing silks for the race was: "Why do I have to ride this horrible horse in this race? I don't stand a chance."

But on the walk to the gate, he decided to be positive. "I hope he's going to surprise me," Laffit told himself.

The race began and once in the backstretch, the horse started to move, yet Laffit remained unimpressed. By the three-eighths pole, however, the horse was closing in on striking distance of the leader. The horse gathered speed and Laffit began to realize he had a chance. Into the home stretch, he worked the horse hard, catching and passing the others and miraculously, Bedouin crossed the finish line. Laffit had won seven races in one day!

When it was over, the roar from those in the stands was deafening. After that, sports writers everywhere not only praised Laffit's success but his ability as a jockey. He lived up to what trainer Buster Millerick once said, "He's so good he almost could ride a pig across the finish line first."[27]

While others celebrated his incredible feat, he put off having a steak and a glass of wine. It was a Saturday and Laffit had important races the next day. He'd been lucky that day, even though he'd indulged the night before. He wouldn't tempt the fates any further.

---

[27] "Laffit Pincay's Winning Touch," Dwight Chapin, *The Los Angeles Times*, June 28, 1974.

The Strike

CHAPTER 22

Jockeys are a playful group of people. Perhaps it's how they counterbalance the gravity of what they do on the racetrack. They like to laugh, and they love to share stories.

"Have you heard the latest Laffit story?" friends would ask. Beyond being a super athlete, Laffit could also be an incredibly funny man—whether he meant to be or not.

Fellow jockeys knew Laffit had a tendency to mix things up sometimes—spraying hairspray on his underarms and deodorant on his hair. He hated carrying the shampoo bottle so he would squirt some on his head (and walk carefully) before heading into the shower.

His small white dickey was frequently forgotten when he stripped down after a race. Occasionally he could be caught in the shower scrubbing up with the dickey still around his neck, completely unaware. Fellow jockeys would watch and wait to see how long it would take for Laffit to catch on, and listen for him to begin yelling in Spanish.

Laffit was also known for taking short naps between races. To make certain he didn't miss a race, he kept a small alarm in his boots to wake himself. One day on his way to the gate he realized he'd forgotten to turn off the alarm, grabbed it from his boot, switched it off and stuck it in his underwear. Seconds before the race was to begin, with all riders on their mounts waiting for the gate to fly open, Laffit's alarm began to ring. He had to dig into his pants with one hand and hold on to the reins with the other—all as the gate opened.

Laffit seemed to forget any number of things. Linda was cleaning out her husband's pockets one day when she discovered a $10,000 check someone had given him weeks earlier. "Oh, I forgot about that," he told her.

Checks weren't the only thing he forgot. Once Linda drove with Laffit to watch the races and afterwards waited patiently for her husband to pick her up outside the jocks' room. After waiting an hour and a half, figuring something had come up, Linda caught a cab home. When the cab pulled up Laffit was franticly pacing in front of their house.

"Where were you?" He yelled at her. "I came home and you weren't here and I couldn't get into the house!" Linda took a deep breath then quietly reminded her husband that he had driven her to the track that morning. Laffit looked blankly at his wife then slapped his forehead with his palm. Immediately contrite, Laffit crooned, "Oh baby, I'm so sorry." He walked up and kissed her on the cheek. "How could I ever forget you? Will you forgive me?" Naturally, she did.

Laffit liked to play prankster off the track as well. He and Bill Shoemaker enjoyed going out on Saturday nights to celebrate their week of winnings. One night they chose to go to Chasen's, a place both of them liked and where the bartender, Pepi, always made sure they were well attended to. One particular evening, when Bill was out of earshot, Laffit enlisted Pepi's help. "We have a big race tomorrow, Pepi, and Shoe's riding the favorite. I need you to help me get him drunk." A wink from Pepi sealed the deal.

Laffit slipped out of Chasen's a little after midnight. He wanted a good night's rest for the next day's race. Bill barely noticed his friend's departure; he was having such a good time telling stories to newly acquired friends at the bar.

In the morning, Laffit received a call from Pepi. "They had to carry Shoemaker out of the restaurant last night. His legs were spread apart so far they had to move him sideways out the door."

Confident that he now was going to win that day's race, Laffit casually walked into the jockeys' room at Santa Anita only to find Bill Shoemaker playing poker with the other jockeys, as sober as could be.

Bill won that day, despite the subterfuge.

As delightful as some of these stories are, some are of a more serious nature. To his fellow jockeys, nothing was more important than what he did for them in the fall of 1988.

Laffit was at the top of his career and scheduled to ride in the inaugural running of the NYRA mile. The purse for that race was an astonishing $500,000 for which the winner would be able to add a handsome up tick to his year's winnings. Laffit was scheduled to ride Forty Niner in that race, one of the favorites for the upcoming Breeders Cup Classic with a purse in the millions. He looked forward to that race as well.

Though a jockeys' strike was threatened, the owner of Forty Niner hoped it would be resolved before the NYRA race. Regardless of the strike situation, the man told Laffit he expected him to ride. If he didn't, he made it clear that they'd still be friends, but he would get another jockey for the Breeder's Cup.

When Laffit arrived in New York, the strike was set to begin. Those jockeys who had not achieved Laffit's superstar status were beginning to argue about the accepted status quo. They wanted more pay for risking their lives and just as importantly, they wanted, indeed desperately needed, adequate medical coverage. The contract they were operating under in 1988 offered minimal care. A jockey who sustained a major injury would have to pay the majority of his medical costs himself. When a jockey couldn't pay those expenses (and most of them couldn't) other jockeys would pitch in to help. It was a haphazard form of insurance, to say the least.

As jockeys, each knew that racing was all about winning. They starved themselves and risked their lives every day, sometimes for as little as thirty-five dollars a mount, hoping to grab the brass ring, to win that big purse and to move up in the standings.

Laffit's work in the stables in Panama had put him in a unique position. He had been where many of the grooms and jockeys were. He distinctly remembered what it was like to be helpless and vulnerable. The past twenty years had offered him the life he had hoped for. He wanted others to have the same opportunity.

Behind the beautiful grandstand at Santa Anita there is a dirt pathway that leads to where the horses are stabled and where the workers live. Horses are housed below, workers sleep above. It is a dusty environment, but at Santa Anita it is better than at many other tracks.

To the rear of the living quarters are a medical trailer, a music trailer, and a chapel trailer. Jockeys are married, serenaded and have their children all in this same succinct block. For them, this small world is a blessing. But it is a world everyone hopes to someday leave when they, like Laffit, make it big.

Laffit was often known to quietly help someone out, to take them to the hospital, to pay their bill, to find someone an apartment and pay for three months rent until that person could get situated. He never wanted anyone to know about it, he merely wanted to help. He felt it was the right thing to do.

So when Laffit entered the jockeys' room at Aqueduct that fall day, he was preparing himself to win an important race aboard Forty Niner. He was also mentally spending the $500,000 prize money he was a sure bet to win.

What he found instead was a room full of despondent jockeys in need of a leader. The group laid out its complaints to Laffit. He was not unfamiliar with their concerns. His position was different, however. Trainers now came to Laffit begging for his services. He no longer had to ride hags for the privilege of earning a pittance. And yet, and yet …

The spokesman for the group turned to Laffit when he was done and asked their hero, "What do we do, Laffit? Should we strike today or not?" There was a long silence as they waited for Laffit's answer. Whether Laffit would stand with this ragtag group was uncertain. If he chose to ride that afternoon, they would lose a powerful voice. They needed him, but Laffit no longer needed the group to fight for his rights. He was beyond that. And yet, and yet …

A jockey, is a jockey, is a jockey is what Laffit always believed. He may have been at the top of the heap, but he was at the top of the heap of jockeys.

Finally Laffit stood up and announced, "I don't know about you, but I'm going shopping."

The group let out a huge scream. Laffit was standing with them! They had star power behind their argument!

Laffit's support that day was never forgotten.

Forty-Niner, the horse Laffit was set to ride that afternoon, was ridden by a scab who won the $500,000 race. Laffit may have lost the purse that day, but he earned far more in the eyes of his fellow jockeys.

JEANINE

CHAPTER 23

In 1988 the fates brought a beautiful woman, barely eighteen years of age, into Laffit's life. Jeanine Dorn and Laffit were introduced at the track by his old friend Humberto. After a flirtatious exchange, the two made a date to have lunch where Laffit confessed to the lovely Jeanine that he was living with someone, but was going to end that relationship. She then told him, "Call me when you're available."

Untangling himself from Phyllis was going to be tricky. Before moving in, Phyllis had insisted on a palimony agreement. At that time, actor Lee Marvin had been in the news when his live-in girlfriend, Michelle Triola, was awarded a hefty settlement when the couple split. Phyllis insisted on an agreement that in the event of a separation, she would be supported by Laffit for a full year. He agreed.

Complicating the split was Phyllis' volatile nature. She had been pushing for marriage; a separation was *not* in her plans. Though he cared for Phyllis, it was not a love match and because of her ongoing problems with his children, it never would be. He knew he had to extricate himself from Phyllis, but because he felt he needed her testimony in the lawsuit against Andrews, he was hesitant.

His mind constantly drifted to Jeanine—those ice blue eyes, that fabulous body, and the sweet way she smiled, drove Laffit wild. For her part, Jeanine had long had a crush on Laffit (even had a poster of him on her bedroom wall) and was equally taken. His being twenty-five years older did not bother her in the least.

Because they couldn't stay apart, nor date out in the open until things were resolved, Laffit and Jeanine occasionally snuck off for dinner to a place where the couple wouldn't be discovered. (Jeanine's resolve not to see him until his was free obviously didn't hold.)

Before long, everyone, save for Phyllis, seemed to know about the relationship. Each week Laffit grew more convinced that his feelings for Jeanine were genuine. He was impressed by how smart she was and how principled. Jeanine, however, made it clear that the relationship was going to be limited until Laffit was separated from Phyllis.

The couple spent one hot afternoon off the beaten track in a motel in El Toro trying to beat the heat just cuddling and talking. Though Laffit hoped for more than kisses, the fact that Jeanine was able to turn away his advances until he was a free man left Laffit delightfully insane.

Laffit's chance to remove Phyllis came not long after when Young Laffit was home from military school, which he described as paradise compared to life at home with Phyllis. The afternoon the boy was due to leave, he was waiting for his aunt to pick him up to take him to the train.

Young Laffit, thirteen-years-old at the time, had not gotten along with Phyllis over the weekend. His father and Phyllis got into an argument over it. When Laffit left to go to the track, an enraged Phyllis barged into the boy's room wielding a knife. "Regardless of anything you say or do, you are not going to split your father and me up." Luckily Aunt Millie arrived, heard about the knife, and quickly whisked Young Laffit off.

Young Laffit later spoke to his dad, "Dad, listen, I've tried to respect her and I respect you, but if she ever comes at me again ...."

Laffit assured his son he was getting out of the relationship.

As luck would have it, that very week Phyllis discovered the credit card bill to the hotel where Laffit had taken Jeannine that hot summer day. Though Laffit had paid in cash, when his credit card was used for identification, the clerk had for some reason run it through. When Phyllis demanded to know if he was seeing someone, Laffit simply said, "Well, you caught me."

After seven years together, even though Laffit knew he was madly in love with Jeanine and that Phyllis and his children would never get along, he felt badly about hurting Phyllis so deeply.

As promised, Laffit helped Phyllis move her things out of the house and supported her for a year.

NEW LOVES

CHAPTER 24

With Phyllis gone, the romance between Jeanine and Laffit blossomed. They were madly in love and before long were talking about marriage. Though Laffit had never intended to remarry, once he'd met Jeanine, he changed his mind. He knew she wanted a full life, one that would include marriage and children and he couldn't deny her. After a year of dating, Laffit proposed. To make certain of their compatibility, and more importantly her compatibility with his children, Jeanine moved in.

Though the children were close in age to Jeanine—Jeanine, at 20, was actually two years younger than Lisa and just three years older than Young Laffit—both were delighted with their father's choice. Young Laffit remarked, "After Phyllis, Dad could have brought home a goat and we'd have been happy."

Jeanine assumed her position as the woman of the house and had her own ideas about how things should be done. Though the children liked Jeanine, the new family unit certainly was not without some adjustments. Wisely, they all went into counseling to help sort through any issues that arose before they became problems. Compromises had to be made by everyone, and they were. Where their mother's photos would hang (in their rooms, not in the den) and how the Thanksgiving turkey would be cooked (Jeanine's method, not Lisa's) were easily resolved.

Overriding everything was the fact that Laffit and Jeanine were madly in love and that joy permeated the house. The couple finally wed in blue jeans on November 29, 1992, at the Silver Bells Chapel in Las Vegas. The bride was twenty-one, the groom was forty-five. Jeanine's mom, step

Wedding in Las Vegas. Young Laffit, Jeanine and Laffit, November 29, 1992

dad and brother came, along with Lisa and Young Laffit. After the ceremony they had dinner at Caesar's Palace and Laffit gave Jeanine's family money to gamble while he and his new bride took Lisa and Young Laffit to play video games until three in the morning.

Laffit's commitment to Jeanine was absolute, unlike any other he had ever made. He vowed to her and to himself to be a completely loyal husband and he kept his promise. He had learned from his past and would never again cause pain to a woman he loved.

He was so reformed that when someone would point out a gorgeous woman, Laffit would reply, "Why would I care about her? My wife is a beautiful woman. I don't need anyone else."

Within months Jeanine became pregnant and the following October, she presented Laffit with a son, Jean-Laffit. Laffit was in the delivery room when his youngest son was born, something he never thought he'd do but Jeanine wanted him there and so he was. He found Jeanine's bravery through the intense labor remarkable and when Jean-Laffit arrived, his father fell madly in love with him.

Jeanine proved herself to be as wonderful a mother as Laffit had anticipated and their little boy grew into an adorable toddler who made them both laugh. Laffit was happy to finally be the kind of father he'd wished he'd been with his grown children and devoted himself fully to his family. Happily, Lisa and Young Laffit doted on their baby brother.

The one subject, and the only one, that set Jeanine off—
and Laffit was careful to avoid it at all costs—was what Laffit referred to as "first wife syndrome." Jeanine did not like
reminders of being his second wife. In fact, she didn't appreciate references to *any* previous wife, whether it was her husband's or someone else's.

Once when Paul McCartney was on television and mentioned his deceased wife, (ironically, whose name was also
Linda) Jeanine went into a rage. "I would divorce that man if
he were my husband!" Jeanine screamed. Laffit tried to be
sensitive to Jeanine's aversion but it sometimes proved difficult. He did have two children by Linda after all. Still, the
topic of first wives was verboten.

Over the years, Laffit would get occasional calls from
Phyllis asking about some of the items she'd left in the house
they'd shared together. Oddly, no concrete arrangement was
ever made to retrieve them until Jean-Laffit was two years-
old, and Phyllis decided to stop by and pick them up.

"Oh what a beautiful baby!" Phyllis gushed over Jean-
Laffit as they all stood in the kitchen. Lisa and Young Laffit
looked on apprehensively. Then Phyllis said, "Oh Laffit, I
found this and wanted to return it to you." She reached into
her purse and pulled something out. "I'm sure you've missed
it," she said, smiling as she handed the item to Laffit. "It's
your little black book."

Laffit was enraged. He knew the gesture was meant to
plant fears in Jeanine's mind and humiliate him in front of

his children. After she left, however, Jeanine simply said, "That was before we were together." The incident didn't faze her in the least, but Laffit vowed never to talk to Phyllis again.

Love revitalized Laffit in many ways. He began riding with a new fervor. He wanted his new wife to experience the good life and before long, Laffit was taking his place again as lead rider. While newcomers were amazed that someone close to fifty could be riding so brilliantly, those who'd been around a while weren't at all surprised. After all, this was Laffit. You never wrote off Laffit.

SPORT, ILLUSTRATED

CHAPTER 25

Laffit was anxious to put a call in to Shoemaker the minute he returned to town. He wanted to share what he'd heard at a benefit in New York for the group that funds the world's largest spinal cord injury research center[28]. Doctors were making remarkable progress. "Just hang in there, Shoe. They're gonna find a cure. You'll see." The news seemed to lift Shoemaker's spirits. Since his injury, it had been hard to watch this formerly stellar athlete reduced to a man in a wheelchair that needed others to do everything for him.

---

[28] The Buoniconti Fund to Cure Paralysis.

Laffit felt guilty that he didn't spend more time with his friend Shoe. He knew he should, but it just was too painful.

Shoe's accident had been a horrible shock to everyone. When it initially happened, the word had been hopeful. Yes, there had been a bad accident and Shoe's car had rolled over but he seemed okay. Some reported that he had been drinking but jockey agent George O'Brien, who had played golf with Shoemaker that afternoon, said he didn't see him drink at all. In fact, a group of them had played liar's poker in the clubhouse and though some people were drinking, Shoe wasn't one of them. (Authorities did conclude, however, that Shoemaker had a blood-alcohol level of .13 at the time of the accident.[29])

Shoemaker was in a playful mood that day. When George won the hundred-dollar pot, Shoe tore the bill in half, then taped it together backwards before he handed it over. O'Brien left his friend at six o'clock and didn't hear the news until hours later. He immediately rushed to the hospital.

Dr. Robert Kerlan, the orthopedic surgeon who was renowned for his work with top athletes, examined Shoe when he arrived at the hospital. Kerlan said the jockey was alert and had full function of his legs and arms. However, an x-ray the doctors ordered was interpreted as showing a pelvic break. They decided to operate. But something happened

---

[29] "Sports People: Horse Racing; Shoemaker Files Suit," *The New York Times*, April 18, 1992

either during or because of the surgery and Shoe left the operating room paralyzed.

Afterwards they realized that what they saw on the x-ray had not been a break after all, but scar tissue from an old injury. It was a horrible tragedy.

Laffit was further upset when the Shoemakers divorced. It was a terrible time for the Shoe to be alone. Seeing his idol in a wheelchair was too heartbreaking and so, regrettably, he stayed away—though he did stay in touch. It was not because he thought, as many did, that Shoe had brought the accident on himself. It was because, in contrast, Laffit's life was flourishing.

The new family: Lisa's husband David, Lisa, Jeanine, Laffit, Jean-Laffit and Laffit III.

The Pincay household was vibrant and Laffit was happier than ever. Jean-Laffit was a delightful boy and Jeanine lavished time and attention on her son and her husband. Laffit was busy at the track and feeling healthier and more energized.

Laffit's new diet had created a remarkable change in his stamina and his moods. After months of agonizing, Laffit finally took some advice about nutrition he'd heard in a television documentary and added fruit to his diet. Any alteration in what he consumed caused justifiable fear on Laffit's part. In the past when he added anything even as simple as a vitamin, he gained weight. The advice had been very specific: only fruits with a skin that could be eaten should be consumed—apples, grapes, pears, etc.

After months of deliberation, Laffit ate a combination of chopped apple, a few blueberries, a bit of peach, some spirulena and a dash of cremora. Within an hour, he felt a sudden boost in his energy level. For some miraculous reason, Laffit discovered that once he added the fruit, he could consume more protein which gave him extra energy. This gave him more strength to ride, which helped him to do even better at the track. It was a win/win situation.

Additionally, though Jeanine enjoyed Laffit's successes, she was not anywhere near as invested as Linda had been in Laffit's winning. Whether he won or lost at the track was irrelevant to her. When Laffit came home, he was just her husband and Jean-Laffit's dad.

Laffit III, Lisa, Jeanine, Jean-Laffit, Laffit, Rosario and friend Berta.

Laffit was more in love than he'd ever been. He had his wife's name tattooed on his right arm.

While at Del Mar one summer day, Laffit was introduced to Academy Award winning producer Jim Wilson, who had won an Oscar for *Dances With Wolves*. Wilson, a horse owner, was a huge fan of Laffit's. He wanted to make a documentary of Laffit's life. Was he interested? Laffit was flattered but when Wilson explained what he wanted to do, which was shoot some of the film in Panama and interview him extensively, he gently declined. "Maybe when I retire," he joked. Laffit needed to stay focused on riding.

Then in 2002, Laffit's agent called to say that the Spanish issue of *Sports Illustrated* was interested in using him in a spread featuring athletes and their beautiful wives. Laffit was the only jockey to be asked.

It was no small surprise that *Sports Illustrated* wanted Jeanine. For years, Jeanine Pincay turned heads. A tall brunette with a perfect model's body, Jeanine was a born pin-up. The only problem Laffit had was convincing Jeanine to do the spread.

"I don't want to be in a swimsuit for all the word to see and have them pick on my imperfections," was Jeanine's response when Laffit told her about the offer. The family was sitting at the kitchen counter having lunch.

It was Jean-Laffit, eight years-old at the time, who changed her mind. "Mom, what do you care what other people think?" And with that vote of confidence, Jeanine nervously agreed.

The actual shoot was terrifying for her, but luckily the photographer provided a bottle of wine which Jeanine and Laffit consumed before the first picture was snapped. There was Laffit in his riding gear, with gorgeous Jeanine in a skimpy swimsuit.

When the magazine came out, however, the Panamanian community was in an uproar. "Too submissive," some complained about Laffit's leaning his head into Jeanine's bosom. They also objected to Jeanine, instead of her husband, holding the riding crop.

But Jean-Laffit was thrilled. He hung the photo of his parents up in his room—until too many of his friends commented on how "hot" his mom was.

The centerfold. "Jeanine was a born pin-up."

Before he could grasp what was happening, Laffit was suddenly in reach of meeting and surpassing Shoemaker's remarkable record of winningest jockey of all time. The phone started ringing off the hook and his agent Bob Meldahl began arranging more and more interviews for his client. With each win, speculation grew as to when the historic event might happen.

Laffit was in the jockeys' room, in the midst of the record push, when he was asked to come to the security office at Santa Anita. Though it was unusual to be summoned there, it was nothing that alarmed Laffit. When he arrived, three men he'd never met before were in the office.

One man extended his hand, "Mr. Pincay, Robert Hammer, FBI."

Laffit nodded a hello. Hammer handed Laffit a picture. "Can you identify the man in this picture?" Hammer asked.

"Sure, that's Ted Aroney," Laffit answered.

"You know him?"

"Yeah, I met him at Sid and Jenny Craig's house. He owns horses and is a friend of theirs. Why?"

"He says you fixed a race for him."

"What?" Laffit was stunned.

"He told us he gave you $65,000 to pull one of the big horses in a race a little while ago."

"I've never fixed anything in my life." Laffit was in shock.

"This guy was pretty clear about it. Said he phoned you on your cell phone and arranged everything."

"Wait a minute, he said he called me?"

"Yep."

"I don't even have his phone number and I never gave him mine."

"He said you talked."

"Well, check the phone records. I never called him and he never called me."

"You're sure of that?"

"Positive. Positive. I never in my life did anything like that. Why would I? Give me a lie detector test if you don't believe me."

There was a pause and then Hammer said,

"Why don't we do that? Why don't you come down and take that test tomorrow?"

"I'm racing tomorrow."

"When are you off?"

"Monday."

"Fine, Monday 10 AM. Here's the address," Hammer handed Laffit a card. The FBI logo was prominent. It made Laffit shudder.

Laffit turned and left, too shaken to say any more.

By the time he got home, Laffit was in full panic mode. He told Jeanine what had happened and luckily, she was very soothing. "You have nothing to worry about. You didn't do anything wrong. You'll take the lie detector test and that will be that."

It calmed Laffit.

"By the way, Mike Mooney called. There are some reporters who want to interview you about breaking the record. They wanted to do it on Monday morning." Mooney was the Hollywood Park publicist Laffit was friendly with.

"Can you call and tell Mike I have a doctor's appointment or something? Whatever you do, don't tell him about all this."

"Don't worry, honey, this will all be over in a couple days.

On the following Monday, Jeanine accompanied Laffit to the Century City offices of the FBI. A receptionist took Laffit's name and asked them both to sit on a wooden bench. In a few minutes, Hammer came out and took Laffit, alone, to the room where they would conduct the test.

Hammer left Laffit in a small room with a table that had the lie detector machine on it. Two men, along with Hammer, went in and out of the room fidgeting with knobs and dials. They explained they would be asking him a series of questions. One of them began to strap Laffit into the device. He could feel himself beginning to panic. *Why is this happening to me?* kept going through his brain. As the minutes dragged on, he began to perspire. Finally, they were ready to begin.

Laffit assumed Hammer would be asking the questions, but Hammer was not in the room when it began. A man at the dials asked Laffit four questions, then he changed the order and asked them again, then again and again and again.

"How long are we going to do this?" Laffit asked the man.

"If you want to stop, just say so." Laffit felt caught. Was this a trick? If he stopped, would they think it meant something?

He told them no, to continue but by now he was completely unnerved. Finally, the man said they were through. He unstrapped Laffit.

Then Hammer came into the room. He stood in front of Laffit.

"Are you satisfied now? Can I go?" Laffit asked.

"Laffit, I'm very disappointed. You've been lying. The test proves it."

Laffit was dumbstruck.

"I'm gonna let you go for now but we'll be in touch. Take him back to the waiting room," he instructed the man who'd conducted the test.

Laffit staggered out of the room and when he spotted Jeanine in the waiting room he signaled for her to follow him. She scurried to join him and blessedly the elevator they entered was empty. The door closed quickly.

"What happened?"

"I flunked the lie detector test."

"What?" Jeanine was shocked.

Laffit began crying.

"What's going to happen to me?"

"Nothing is going to happen. You didn't do anything. They can't prove a damn thing."

Laffit was silent the rest of the ride down but his brain was churning. *I have to get a lawyer. This is going to cost a fortune.* And then it came to him, *Oh my god, the record!* Just at a time when he was the focus of more publicity than he had ever received in his life, this kind of news threatened to break and ruin everything.

"Give me the car keys. I'll drive," Jeanine offered.

They both decided that nothing should be said about what was going on. Each day, Laffit went to the track, chasing the record, staying focused on the races ahead of him and pushing the FBI out of his head.

He desperately wanted to call Ted Aroney and confront him but thought better of it. It might only complicate things.

Meanwhile, he was riding brilliantly. Still, each day he scoured the paper, fearful he might find some reference to him and the FBI. After a lifetime of being an upstanding citizen and a sportsman with an impeccable record, Laffit couldn't believe he was in the position of maybe having to defend himself against a false allegation.

The record was tantalizingly close. Hotels and motels were taking reservations for reporters from all over the world. On a daily basis, Laffit was posing for pictures, answering questions, doing interviews. The excitement was building, as was his internal panic.

One afternoon the FBI came knocking at the Pincay home. Hammer had a deal to offer Laffit.

"If you testify against Aroney, we will go easy on you."

"Forget it," Laffit firmly told him.

"I have to tell you, if you don't take this offer, we're going to offer it to Aroney. "

"Have you even bothered to check the phone records? If you did, you'd know that I had never called him."

"Last chance, Laffit. This is a good deal. You sure you don't want to take it?"

"I am not going to admit to anything I didn't do. Ever."

When Hammer left, Laffit turned to Jeanine. "I don't think he has anything on me."

She was surprised. "What makes you think that?"

"If he did, why would he be offering me a deal? He knows I didn't do anything. If he did, he would arrest me."

The weeks dwindled down to days and before they knew it, Laffit was on the precipice of becoming the winningest jockey of all time. Jeanine worried that she didn't have anything new to wear for the special event, then realized they wouldn't know exactly when that day would be anyway, and stopped fretting. Hollywood Park prepared for a massive celebration and during those final days, when it was within his grasp, six-year-old Jean-Laffit was allowed to play hooky from school.

Shoemaker came to the track on December 9, 1999, the day they thought it might happen. Shoemaker had broken Johnny Longden's record in 1970. It had been almost thirty years since Shoemaker had done it and no one but Laffit had even come close. Shoemaker was delighted to cheer his friend along, even if it meant relinquishing his own record.

Excitement built in the jocks' room as his fellow riders watched the televised races and cheered Laffit onward. A phalanx of reporters and a crush of camera crews followed Laffit from the jockeys' room to the paddock, then back to the scale. It was the kind of attention that made Laffit dizzy.

Finally the moment arrived. He had lost the first three races that fateful day but I Be Casual proved anything but. It was a photo finish. From where Jeanine and the family stood they couldn't tell, but happily Laffit won by a nose. He'd matched Shoemaker's record! Now he had to beat it.

A mob scene awaited the athlete in the winner's circle. He was draped in a blanket of yellow flowers and fellow Panamanian Omar Berrio handed Laffit a Panamanian flag that Laffit carried for the photo. The crowd in the stands gave Laffit a standing ovation. The flash from photographer's cameras was blinding.

The tension was massive on everyone's part. Laffit was scheduled to ride five mounts the next day, Friday. Everyone would be back for the big event.

Laffit with Bill Shoemaker.

It was not easy for Shoemaker to travel back and forth, needing the kind of care he did, nor was it easy for Lisa, Laffit's daughter. She had given birth to Laffit's first grandchild, Madelyn, called Maddy, just one month before. This was a family affair though, and Lisa wanted the baby there. She would witness her grandfather's victory, even if she'd never remember it. Young Laffit—by now taking on the more mature moniker of Laffit III—was working in New York as a sport's announcer. His younger brother, Jean-Laffit was ready to celebrate. JL (as he was referred to by friends) was delighted to be missing school though he wasn't exactly sure what all the fuss was about. No one had taken the time to explain it to him.

Beating Shoemaker's record, December 10, 1999 on Irish Nip

The day finally came and on December 10, 1999. Laffit rode Irish Nip to a victory that was wire-to-wire. It was win number 8,834 on his 44,647[th] ride.

The celebration – Laffit and Jean-Laffit are hoisted. Roseann and Humberto can be seen in the background on the left.

Fellow jockeys lifted Laffit and Jean-Laffit on their shoulders as champagne was uncorked and lights flashed. "When I saw the numbers on the tote board, then I figured it out," Jean-Laffit said with a grin.

Jeanine, Laffit and Laffit III after the win.

A celebration followed which included the presentation of a white Porsche with a license plate reading 8834, a gift from four Southern California race tracks. It was driven onto the track by jockey Chris McCarron. Rousing tributes were read, and fellow jockeys, including Bill Shoemaker, extolled his amazing talent. "Laffit has conducted himself with dignity all through his career, he's had ups and downs and he never gave up."[30]

Listening to tributes.

The victory celebration had to be cut short, however. Laffit was set to ride another horse, Storm Dog, and had to change silks. It was back to business for the working jockey.

Ironically, he lost that race.

Months later Laffit called Hammer to find out what was happening with the case that continued to keep him up at night.

---

[30] "Pincay Breaks Shoe's All-time Winning Mark," *The Chicago Sun Times*, December 11, 1999.

"Oh, we dropped that case. We put a tail on the guy for a bunch of illicit stuff. We found out he was a bookie. We think he was just bragging that he could buy you to throw a race.

You're all clear."

THE FALL

CHAPTER 26

He had broken his collarbone thirteen times, his ribs ten times, suffered three broken thumbs, two punctured lungs, two spinal fractures and three fractured ankles but nothing, nothing, prepared him for March 1, 2003.

If he'd been scheduled to ride nine horses that day he'd have told his agent to take him off Trampus Too, but he was only set for eight, so he said nothing. He was happy to be so busy.

It was the Santa Anita Handicap and there was big money to be made that day. When the fifth race was about to start, the six and a half turf furlong, Laffit was pleased that Trampus Too felt composed under him as he sat at the starting gate. Earlier he'd been concerned. The horse wasn't necessarily dangerous, just difficult to control. He liked to lug in—lean his head to the inside, often in the path of other horses—and Laffit didn't want to get suspended if he somehow had trouble keeping the horse in check. It was a good sign that Trampus Too kept his nose on the gate, focused on the path ahead of him.

Once the bell went off, the horse began to advance quickly, jumping into third position and then pouncing into second. Laffit's blood began to pump. The horse was obeying his commands. He had a good shot at the win, he could sense it.

They were coming into the patch that connected the turf with the track, a tricky crossover for horses because the ground adjustment was often hard for them to make. As they raced down that hillside turf, on the turn to home, Laffit saw Rainman's Request moving toward him on his left. The horse swung wide, dangerously close to cutting him off. Laffit sought Tony Farina's eye but the jockey stayed focused straight ahead. Laffit quickly lifted the reins firmly, using all his strength to pull his horse back, but there was not enough time.

Rainman's Request sliced in front and Trampus Too—trapped—clipped the other horse's heels. As though shot from a cannon, Laffit was immediately thrust high into the air and over the neck of his horse. He landed with a heavy thud onto the ground, his head smacking the turf. Trampus Too stumbled. Laffit's left eye then caught sight of the twelve hundred pound horse coming down fast on him, the horse's eyes frantic with fear. There was no time for Laffit to move. When the horse rolled onto him, the wind exploded out of his chest.

For interminable seconds, he could not breathe, could not move. He lay suspended in some ether land, unable to connect with himself or what had happened. The horse beside him whinnied its distress but Laffit could not help the horse. He could not move, could not even smell the beloved turf beneath him.

Then he heard the approach of the ever-present ambulance. The race was suspended while all eyes focused on the downed jockey. Despite his pain, Laffit's only thought was of Jeanine. She was in the Front Runner Restaurant that day to watch the Handicap.

He had often warned her not to worry when she saw a jockey lying on the ground. Most of the time they got up within minutes and were fine, he'd told her. But this time, he couldn't get up.

The paramedics bent over him and asked how he was. "I have a lot of pain on the left side of my neck," he told them, "but I don't want my wife to worry. Help me stand up." Two men helped him up and Laffit wobbled around to the back of the ambulance.

When he got to the rear of the vehicle, he was grateful to be helped in. The pain coming from his neck was blinding. He was anxious to find out what was wrong.

The ride to the first aid center took only minutes but seemed agonizingly long and painfully bumpy. Remarkably, Jeanine had already made her way down to the first aid center by the time they pulled up, minutes later. His son, Laffit III was there as was Jean-Laffit.

"Sweetheart, are you okay?" Jeanine was leaning over Laffit, a worried look in her eyes.

"I'm going to be fine. Don't worry. It's nothing serious. You saw me walking, right?"

At that moment, a man in a white smock approached them.

"I hear you had a spill. How are you doing?"

"My neck really hurts."

The man in white moved Laffit on to the examining table and then had him sit up. Laffit grunted from the exertion of the move.

"Where exactly is the pain?"

"On the left side of my neck, here." Laffit, eyes closed, told the man, pointing.

The doctor held Laffit's neck and twisted it abruptly to the far right.

"Ow!" Laffit cried out. "That hurt!"

The doctor then twisted his head to the left. The pain was excruciating. Laffit's face drained of all color.

"I think I'm going to faint." Laffit put his head in his hands. "I need to lie down."

After a few minutes Laffit's breathing began to steady, but his eyes were darting around the room.

"What's wrong with my neck?" he wanted to know, "it's so painful."

"You have a little strain. I don't think you have anything to worry about. I'll give you some pain medication, but I don't think you should ride for a couple of days."

"A little strain?" Jeanine asked. "This is more than a little strain. Shouldn't we get him x-rayed?" She knew that if Laffit was complaining of any kind of pain, it had to be bad.

"A few days rest and he'll be as good as new."

She looked at her husband. His face was contorted.

"I don't know," Jeanine said.

"Get him home and give him one of these pills." The doctor handed Jeanine a prescription. "They'll help with the pain."

With the boys help, they somehow made it home. They got Laffit upstairs, but it took considerable time. He needed to stop after each step to recover from the exertion. When they finally got to their room, Jeanine undressed her husband and washed his hands and face as he sat on the side of the bed. He was still covered with dirt from the fall. She knew how much that usually bothered him, though today he didn't seem to care. He simply wanted to lie down. Jeanine carefully held his back and helped lower him onto the raised pillows. Laffit III ran to the pharmacy to have the prescription filled; Jeanine desperately wanted him to have some relief.

That night Laffit was tired beyond anything he'd every known. He gratefully took the pills when Jeanine brought them to him, hoping they'd help him get a good night's rest. He drifted in and out for hours, but never really slept and in the middle of the night, when he needed to get up to use the bathroom, he found he couldn't move. He woke Jeanine.

"I can't get out of bed," he told her.

Without her, he was helpless.

The pills helped numb the throbbing but didn't eliminate the pain. The next morning Laffit still couldn't move his head from side to side. Friends, as well as family, called voicing concerns.

"No, I'm doing fine. Just a little headache," Laffit lied. "I'll be back in a couple days."

Sleep was impossible, even with the drugs—something Laffit normally would never take. He spent the day in a slightly drugged state, grateful for the semi-relief.

Jeanine was growing anxious.

"Laffit, we have to take you to the hospital for a x-ray. This pain isn't right. Please let me take you. *I'll* feel better. Please."

Jeanine begged, but Laffit told her he just needed to rest.

Privately though, his fears were beginning to mount.

By Monday, Laffit decided he should just push through the pain, something he had done countless times in the past.

"Jeanine, I need you to drive me to the Rose Bowl. I want to walk the track."

"Are you crazy? Laffit, you can barely walk to the bathroom."

"If you don't drive me, I'll drive myself."

"I should drive you to the hospital."

Fearing he would indeed drive himself, Jeanine took them both to the Rose Bowl. She didn't want Laffit driving while on Vicodin.

As they walked the track, Jeanine watched her husband out of the corner of her eye. His normally smooth brow was furrowed and the color of his face was ashen. After one lap, Laffit stopped. Jeanine was relieved.

When they returned from Pasadena, Laffit went into the den and mounted the wooden horse he used for training. It resembled a full-sized horse, and was equipped with reins and a saddle and allowed a rider to put both feet in the stirrups and bounce up and down, simulating a race.

"Laffit, I don't think this is a good idea."

"I'm fine."

"No, you're not."

Laffit rode the horse for ten minutes as Jeanine stood frozen in the doorway watching him wince with pain every time his body came down. She was grateful when the pain in his head made him stop.

He slept even less that night. She didn't sleep much either.

Tuesday morning, Laffit was scheduled to work a horse for trainer Bill Spawr.

"Laffit, you have to call and cancel. You've got no business getting on a horse."

"I told him I'd walk his horse."

"How are you going to mount a horse in the shape you're in?"

"I can do it."

"You're so stubborn."

Luckily, Spawr called and canceled. Later Laffit spoke with his agent, Bob Meldahl, who called asking Laffit how he was doing. "I'm fine," he lied. He decided to get a massage.

Laffit again refused Jeanine's pleadings about getting an x-ray and spent another sleepless night in pain.

The next day Laffit's good friend Alex Solis told him that he should get an x-ray.

"Please, Laffit. What harm can it do? Remember the fracture I had last year? The doctors didn't notice that right away either."

Whether he was worn down by the pain or everyone's pleading, or his own fears, Laffit finally agreed to go.

Jeanine drove them to Arcadia Methodist Hospital. The staff there were used to treating Santa Anita's jockeys and knew Laffit. Jeanine explained to the nurses what had happened and they summoned a doctor who quickly orders x-rays. The head of E.R., Dr. Russell Maatz, was on duty that day even though he was scheduled to be off.

Laffit and Jeanine sat in a cubicle waiting for half an hour for the doctor to return with the results. The pungent smell of a hospital always made Laffit nauseated. Waiting this day, he wasn't sure if it was pain, fear, or the medicinal smells that were making him feel ill.

Finally Laffit looked up, drawn to the sound of hard heels moving toward him. The slumped way Doctor Maatz walked toward Laffit told him everything he didn't want to know. The somber face, the downcast eyes, the plodding feet, the one hand thrust in the white jacket pocket, the other gripping the x-ray as he strode Laffit's way, gave him a sickening feeling in the pit of his stomach.

He entered the room solemnly and locked eyes with the jockey.

"Don't move, Mr. Pincay. I'm going to get you a neck brace. *Do not move!*"

When he left Laffit asked Jeanine, "What's going on?"

"I don't know," she replied.

The doctor was back within a minute.

He began wrapping a soft foam brace around Laffit's neck.

"What's this for?" Laffit asked. "What's wrong with me? What did the x-ray say?"

When it was fastened the doctor said, "This is just temporary."

Jeanine was growing concerned.

"What's wrong with my husband?"

"I'm afraid he has a broken neck."

Laffit was shocked. "A broken neck? Are you sure?"

"I'm very sure. When did you say you had your fall?"

Jeanine told him. Five days ago.

The doctor shook his head. "I'm going to call in a neurologist to take over from here." "You're a very, very lucky man, Mr. Pincay, very lucky indeed."

The doctor left.

"I can't believe it," Laffit was in shock.

"Me, either. I thought if you had a broken neck you couldn't move."

"That's what I thought, too."

"Oh, Laffit, my poor baby. All this time, I'm so sorry."

Laffit gave Jeanine a half smile. "I guess I should have listened to you, huh?"

When the neurologist arrived, he said nothing and instead focused on the x-rays on the wall. He barely looked at Laffit who, though exhausted from pain, was alert for what the doctor would say. Finally he turned to them.

"Mr. Pincay, Mrs. Pincay, I'm Dr. Withers. How are you feeling, Laffit?"

"I've been better."

"I bet you have. I'm sure Doctor Maatz told you that your neck is broken."

"Yeah, he did. I'm a little surprised."

"Well, your neck is broken, but not just in one place. It's broken in three places."

Laffit and Jeanine were dumbstruck.

"How long ago was your fall?"

"Five days." Jeanine told the man.

"Five days and this is the first you're coming in?"

Jeanine lowered her eyes.

The doctor held up the x-ray. "I've never seen anything like this before. I don't know how you've been able to stand." The doctor shook his head.

"How have you been sleeping?"

"Not very well. I have a pretty bad headache all the time."

"I would suspect so."

"What happens now?"

"A broken neck is a very critical injury. Mr. Pincay. It is potentially life threatening. The only way we can stabilize your neck is to put you in a surgical halo. Do you know what a halo is?"

Laffit knew all too well. Richard Migliore, a fellow jockey, had one and Laffit heard it was a horrible experience for him.

"Do we have to?" Laffit asked.

"As unpleasant as the halo is, Mr. Pincay, it's a far better alternative to being in a wheelchair for the rest of your life.

272 - THE FALL

Even the slightest movement could cause permanent paraly-sis."

"It could?" Laffit asked.

"You're lucky it didn't already happen, especially in five days. I hope you've just been staying in bed."

Jeanine spoke up, "No."

The doctor shook his head.

"You're a walking miracle."

Bill Shoemaker raced into Laffit's mind. The Shoe hadn't been lucky, at least in this regard. Such a special man, an extraordinary athlete and now—because he was para-lyzed—he was dependent, since his car accident, on others. It was a fate no man, no athlete, wanted.

"I have to go get a few things," the doctor said. "Don't move."

Jeanine hurried out to call Roseann, a woman she had come to rely upon, to tell her the news and to ask her to call the family. Laffit waited in silence until they returned. He needed a minute to process what he'd just been told. Within minutes Jeanine and the doctor were back, this time the doc-tor brought a nurse and a stainless tray with a lot of equip-ment.

"Right now I'm going to make some marks on your head where the pins will go and then I'll give you some numbing medicine," the doctor explained. He used a special pen to dot Laffit's skull in four places. He then injected each spot.

"This should help somewhat but I have to warn you, it's not pleasant getting a halo put on, but it's entirely necessary.

Please try and stay very steady, don't move your head until I return. Mrs. Pincay, you might want to wait in the waiting room until we're done."

"That's all right. I'm staying with my husband."

Laffit could sense she was nervous.

Paralyzed! Could there be a worse fate for an athlete, unable to do what he loved? Laffit then and there determined he would just have to endure whatever this was so he could get back on a horse. He'd been in pain before. He would somehow have to surmount this and get well.

The doctor brought in a rolling tray with instruments that looked positively medieval.

"What we have to do, Laffit, is lock your neck in place so that it can't move. In order to do that, I will attach these bolts to your head and then screw the bolts to the halo, like this." The doctor held the pieces in his hands and showed Laffit how the attachment would connect.

"I'll start with the two bolts that will go on either side of your head, then I'll add the ones to the back here. I want to avoid your temples so you don't have any scars." The doctor tapped Laffit's head on either side in the rear. "Are you ready?"

"As ready as I'll ever be, I guess. Jeanine, you don't have to stay for this."

"No, I'm staying right with you."

They started with the left side. In what felt like a form of torture, the doctor screwed the bolt into Laffit's skull, just in front of his left ear. Blood immediately began dripping down his cheek and neck onto the chair he was sitting on. Every movement terrified him. The smell of blood filled the room. The nurse held a large wad of gauze to the point of entry and it quickly needed to be replaced. She flung the used pads onto the steel tray at her side and grabbed another. She continued this until the tray was covered in bloody rags.

"Why isn't the numbing medicine working?" Laffit asked the doctor.

"I'm sorry. It doesn't do a perfect job."

Out of the corner of his eye, Laffit could see Jeanine's furrowed brow. He knew that expression. She was feeling sick to her stomach. He was going to tell her to leave but a wave of nausea came over him. Then the doctor took what looked like a hand drill and bore a hole into the bone of his forehead. From then on the pain entered a zone unlike any Laffit had ever experienced.

When the doctor finally finished one side, he swiveled his chair to the right and began all over again.

"You have to stop," Laffit said. "This is too painful."

Jeanine sucked in her breath. In all their years together she'd never heard her husband say anything was too painful. The sight of blood running down his face didn't help. On top of that, she was terrified he'd somehow move the wrong way and be paralyzed.

"I know this is hard, Laffit," the doctor said.

"Just give me a minute."

"Jeanine, honey, can you get me some water?"

"Sure." She was gone in a flash.

"I don't want my wife to have to see this."

"I think she wants to be with you, Laffit," The doctor replied.

Jeanine brought him back the water. She had found a straw, so he wouldn't have to tip his head back to drink.

"Take all the time you need," the doctor told Laffit.

"Roseann and Humberto are out there." Jeanine told Laffit. He gave her a rueful smile.

"Why don't you go keep them company?" he suggested.

She just shook her head no.

After a few minutes, Laffit was ready to continue. They shaved the small spots where the bolts would go. The rear bolts were not as painful. When all the bolts were finally in (the procedure took over an hour) the doctor lifted up the metal halo and carefully began to attach it in place with special screws. As they were twisted in, Laffit felt the slight movements that accompanied the doctor's actions. They terrified him.

The nurse meanwhile was discarding the used bandages and wiping the tray down with a substance that smelled like disinfectant. Laffit saw Jeanine take a Kleenex from her purse and discreetly cover her nose.

Laffit saw his reflection in the glass cabinet behind where the doctor was working. With each minute, he looked more and more like Frankenstein's monster. He was still in shock, but he was glad it was done, over. He just wanted to go home.

When the doctor finally finished, he gave Laffit a pain pill and warned him that his head would hurt until it made the adjustment to the halo.

"I'm really tired. Can I go home now?" His shirt was covered with blood. He desperately wanted to change it.

"I'm afraid we're going to need you to stay here in the hospital so we can monitor how you're doing. That way we can make any adjustments that need to be made."

Laffit closed his eyes. He tried to calm himself. The last thing he wanted to do was stay in the hospital.

"How long will he need to stay, doctor?" asked Jeanine.

"Probably two days is all. Then he should be ready to go home."

"Will I be able to stay with him in his room?"

"If you want, sure. We'll get you a chair that opens up."

"Can I bring our family in to see Laffit now?" Jeanine asked the doctor and he agreed. The look on everyone's face told Laffit all he needed to know about his new appearance. Humberto saw Laffit and immediately lowered his eyes. "Hey, Dad," Laffit III said and went pale when his father returned his gaze. Lisa and Roseann had tears in their eyes. His agent Bob told him he looked fine, while his brother Juan joked with him. Jean-Laffit was the only one not there. He asked his mom if it would be okay to wait in the car and she said yes.

They moved Laffit to a room and Jeanine ran back to the house to get him the things she knew he would want: his cashmere robe, his lamb's wool slippers, and his toiletries.

She was about to toss some t-shirts in his leather overnight bag when she realized there was no way he would be wearing his usual tops for a long, long while.

When she returned less than an hour later, Laffit was in his room and the nurse was bringing in a tray of food.

"Here you go, Mr. Pincay. Some lovely beef stroganoff."

"I can't eat that. Take it away."

The woman looked to Jeanine for guidance.

"Laffit, darling, eat. Please."

He was irritated. "I can't eat this stuff, Jeanine. I'm just going to be sitting for weeks and can't exercise. I'll get fat. You know that."

"You need food."

"I just told you, I have to watch my weight!"

"Why? So you can get on a horse again and get yourself killed?" They were both shocked by Jeanine's vitriol but she was angry.

The nurse quietly slipped out of the room.

His wife slumped against the wall, drained. Why was he so stubborn?

Her voice came out in a whisper. "Laffit, the doctor told me you'll never ride again." She paused. "You might as well eat."

Laffit turned his gaze to the window. It took a moment for the news to register.

"He's wrong. I will ride. Take this tray away."

Jeanine sighed heavily, then walked to the bed and lifted the tray. When she turned to leave, Laffit noticed her eyes, brimming with tears.

"Tell them I want a treadmill here, too."

Two days later, Laffit was going home. They were both delighted. The hospital stay had been hard and Laffit had still not slept, despite the medications they had given him. For Jean-Laffit it was the first time he'd seen his father in the halo. His young imagination had envisioned the screws in the halo going all the way through his father's head. He was relieved when he saw they didn't. "He looked kinda cool," he said, "We started calling him Robocop."

That afternoon, the doctor sent a technician over to the house to tighten the screws. When the man left, the sides of Laffit's head felt like someone was driving spikes into his skull, on top of which, the sites where the bolts were placed were beginning to swell. Laffit alternated feeling he might faint or vomit though luckily he did neither.

He couldn't sleep that night and Jeanine, mercifully, stayed up with him, trying to soothe him in small ways. She rubbed his back and feet and made him his favorite herbal tea, appropriately called Tension Tamer. They turned on the television at 3:00 AM hoping for something to distract him. Nothing worked. The pain was greater than any he'd every known.

At 6 AM the following day, Monday, Jeanine called the doctor's answering service.

"My husband is in excruciating pain. Please have the doctor call me immediately. Something has to be done to help him."

Within the hour, the doctor called and said he would come by the house right away.

The side screws, the doctor determined, were causing the problem. He removed them and placed new ones on either side of Laffit's forehead, and the relief was immediate. The fact that more holes were dug into his skull, or that major amounts of blood were pouring down his face, didn't matter to Laffit. He could breathe again. "You better not bleed all over our new bedspread," Jeanine teased him.

Despite the phenomenal exhaustion, and the heavy duty pain pills, Laffit still could not sleep—could not get comfortable. Finally in the middle of the night (now the eighth night without sleep), Laffit asked Jeanine to bring him a towel. He rolled the towel into a tight wad and stuck it behind his neck and in front of back of the halo. The towel created a soft cushion which was enough to give Laffit some comfort. Finally, finally, he drifted off to sleep.

The healing was agonizingly slow. Fearful of what the first doctor told him—that he might not be able to ride again—Laffit decided he had to find the best neurologist in town for a second opinion.

That week the phone rang constantly. Friends from Panama called, Bill Shoemaker phoned, fellow jockeys, family and friends all checked in often. Some had heard rumors that Laffit was refusing treatment, rumors he quickly squelched. Everyone offered encouragement and suggestions of doctors for him to see. The consensus seemed to be that UCLA had the best neurologist, Dr. Rick Delamarter. Jeanine made an appointment for Laffit to see him.

Jeanine and Laffit drove to Westwood two weeks later to meet with Dr. Delamarter at his office on Santa Monica Boulevard. The doctor was calm and assured. They trusted him immediately.

Laffit humorously asked, "So, doctor, when can I ride again? I'm getting sick of being in this thing."

"I wish I knew, Laffit. I looked at your x-rays very, very carefully. As you know you have three bad breaks."

"That's what they keep saying."

"I'm afraid you have at least another seven or eight weeks before we can safely take the halo off."

"Seven weeks?"

"That's just a guess. It may be longer. I know this isn't what you want to hear, but my job is to protect you and help you to heal and I have to warn you, at your age, and with that kind of break, it may be that your riding days are over."

Jeanine glanced sideways at Laffit to gauge his reaction.

"I know that must be very hard to hear but I have to prepare you, Laffit. I won't really be able to tell until we take off the halo to see how you've healed. Then I'll know for sure."

Laffit slumped in the green chair in the examining room.

They rode back to Arcadia in silence, both Jeanine and Laffit privately replaying the doctor's words in their heads.

Each knew this was always a possibility with horse racing, that any one race could be the last. But this one came at a time when things were so ripe. The slump Laffit had endured years earlier was finally over. His health was better than ever. His marriage was terrific and his young son had brought new meaning to his life.

Why now? he asked the gods.

He works so hard, he loves racing so much, how could this be taken from him? Jeanine questioned.

There was no answer. It simply was.

The next weeks were spent enduring. The pain in his head eventually subsided and Laffit took it as a sign that he was healing, and would be able to ride again soon.

But privately, his older children, Lisa and Laffit III, along with Jeanine, all worried together. Even if the doctors gave him the go-ahead, was riding at the age of fifty-six, when he had just suffered a broken neck, worth the risk they wondered? Jean-Laffit however, sided with his dad. He understood his desire to ride.

They all wanted Laffit to be happy, to do what he loved doing … but the adults asked, at what price? Was the momentary thrill worth the colossal risk? There was no doubt that this was a family that loved him. As hard as it would be for Laffit to not ride again, it would be twenty times harder if Laffit wound up in a wheelchair, dependent on others. His family desperately wanted to prevent a tragedy.

"It's not the end of the world if you don't ride again, you know." Jeanine was trying gently to prepare him, just in case.

"What are you talking about?"

"We have a great life. We have all kinds of things we can do."

"I'm a jockey. *That's* what I do. I can't give up horse-racing."

"You heard what the doctor said. You might have to. He told you that a broken neck is very dangerous."

"I'll heal. I always do. You'll see." He walked off.

It was how many conversations ended lately, in a stale-mate.

On the day the halo was to come off, Laffit was grateful to finally be at the end of this journey. It was longer than the seven weeks the doctors had first predicted. It took ten weeks in all. Though in no pain, Laffit took two Vicodin pills before they left the house. He'd heard how painful it was for Richard Migliore when they took the pins out of his skull, untwisting the screws out of the bone. He wanted to be well-medicated before it happened to him.

The nurse ushered Laffit and Jeanine into a large, sunny room after Laffit had been x-rayed. The excitement Laffit was feeling over having the halo removed dimmed his fears of the actual unbolting. He could feel the pills kicking in. The pills, and his ability to withstand major pain, plus the thrill of finally being healed, fortified him. Or so he thought.

Dr. Delamarter began in the front in the area Laffit imagined would be the least painful. What he was not pre-pared for was that his skin had grown over the bolts and the only way to remove them was to tear the flesh away. He had been told by the doctor that the procedure would be fairly painless. It wasn't.

When the first pin was removed, Laffit felt lightheaded. Then he fainted.

Somehow he endured the other three removals, but his head throbbed terribly.

The real pain that day, however, wasn't physical. After the halo was off, a nurse ushered them into Dr. Delamarter's sleek office overlooking the busy boulevard. Laffit now had bandages where his bolts had been. The bleeding had finally stopped. After a few minutes, the doctor appeared.

"Laffit, I looked at the x-rays we took when you came in here today and you've healed remarkably well." The doctor sat down behind his desk.

"See, Jeanine, I told you." Laffit grinned at his wife.

"It is good news. But that being said, as your doctor, I'm going to tell you what I'd tell you if you were my son, or my best friend or my brother." He directed himself to Laffit.

"I know this is not what you want to hear, but you shouldn't ride again, Laffit. At your age, after these kinds of breaks, it's too dangerous. It's not worth the risk."

Laffit sat there stunned

"You're a lucky man. You have a beautiful family that loves and needs you. You have to think of them right now, Laffit. My advice is not to ride, not ever again. I'm sorry. I wish I had better news."

The doctor stood and walked over to Laffit and patted him on the shoulder.

"This is a lot to absorb, I know. I'll give you two a minute."

Laffit hung his throbbing head. So this is how it ends, he thought—not on the back of a horse, not in front of the crowds, not with the smell of the turf under him—but in a doctor's office.

Somehow he'd never imagined a finish line like the one he'd just crossed.

THE WAITING ROOM

CHAPTER 27

I f ever a miracle could be documented, it was Laffit's brush with death, or at the very least, paralysis. The following were each life-threatening possibilities for a man with a neck broken in three places. The compounding of the events made the situation that much more perilous:

1. The ambulance drivers let him stand up.
2. No actual doctor was at the track to properly evaluate him. The man who greeted him at first aid dressed in a white smock turned out not to be an M.D..

3. The supposed "doctor" severely twisted his neck over the broken area not once, but twice.

4. The "doctor" prescribed an anti-inflammatory drug—the very medicine that can trigger paralysis, as it can cause bleeding from the bone, where Laffit had three breaks.

5. He walked the track at the Rose Bowl, which caused additional vibrations in the neck.

6. He rode the practice horse at home, bouncing his neck up and down.

7. The regular massage he had with a sports masseuse focused on kneading the pain in his neck, again the very area that was broken.

Any one of these things alone could have crippled or killed Laffit, the fact that he survived all of them is a true miracle.

Dr. Maatz, the head of the emergency room, was not scheduled to be at the hospital that day but was, which constitutes another miracle because he knew how to treat these kinds of injuries. Maatz claims that when Laffit walked into the emergency room that afternoon, his neck was hanging by the thinnest of threads. The only thing keeping his neck in place were his strong muscles—plus the huge swelling that occurred when the neck broke. If that swelling had gone down, he claims, the break could very easily have done permanent damage, including the possibility that Laffit's lungs may have stopped working altogether.

And so the final entry on the miracle list is:

8. Timing—Laffit got to the hospital just in the nick of time. Another few hours and the swelling may have gone down and it could have been all over.

During the drilling of the holes into Laffit's scalp, a crowd of family and friends began to fill the emergency room. Jeanine phoned Roseann, sobbing, telling her what they were about to do. A chill ran down Roseann's spine.

The day of the fall, Roseann had an eerie experience she had told no one about. As Jeanine and she and Laffit III's girlfriend were settling in for lunch in the clubhouse, she suddenly thought she caught the strong scent of Linda. She turned around abruptly, anxious to find the source but couldn't. Linda had a characteristic aroma unlike anyone else's. Roseann turned to Laffit III's girlfriend and asked if she had perfume on. The girl replied no. She asked her if she smelled anything? No, the girl said. The fragrance lingered in the air until the fateful race began, then suddenly disappeared. When she heard the news about the halo, she couldn't help but wonder if Linda had been there that day.

Everyone in the racing world knew that a halo was the kiss of death for a jockey. "Will you call everyone and tell them we're at the hospital?" Jeanine asked. Roseann did so immediately.

Roseann first called Laffit III. Laffit III was now an accomplished sports announcer covering horse racing who enjoyed a warm, comfortable relationship with his father. Twenty-seven years of age, he also had a fine appreciation of his father's skills. Being in the business meant he was exposed to many people who shared remarkable stories with him about his father. He was extremely proud to be Laffit Pincay III. More than anything though, he loved his father—not as the jockey that the rest of the world revered, but as his dad.

Roseann, Lisa and Jeanine.

But he was also a young man who had tragically also lost one parent. He did not want to lose another. For Roseann, Linda's oldest friend, the pain of that suicide resurfaced all over again. She had tried her best over the years, along with Millie, to help mother Linda's children in whatever small way she could to bring them comfort. Now, unbelievably, she had to comfort them about their father.

Roseann called Lisa to tell her the news. She wasn't sure how Lisa would react.

Lisa and Laffit had not spoken in almost a year, a turn of events that upset both of them, and deeply upset Roseann. In retrospect, the rapprochement was perhaps inevitable and also probably what ultimately saved their relationship.

As Lisa came to maturity and became a mother herself, she was left with some tough questions she needed her father to answer regarding her mother and some of the things Lisa had witnessed as a young child. Lisa was just a teenager when her mother died but she had many clear and sometimes confusing memories that needed explanation.

Jean-Laffit, Laffit and Lisa's daughter, baby Maddy

Laffit, however, was not anxious to go back in time and revive painful memories. When Laffit refused to talk, Lisa withdrew.

Ironically enough, the morning of that fateful fall, Laffit received a letter in the mail from Lisa. It was an olive branch. After reading it, Laffit told Jeanine, "I want to call her as soon as I get back from the track." He left the letter by the phone as a reminder.

Lisa assured Roseann she was on her way.

In the waiting room, Roseann passed along what facts she knew to Humberto and Neil Papiano, Laffit's friend and attorney. Slowly, as word spread, others gathered.

There was a mournful air in the waiting room of the hospital that day. A sense that it was all over—the years of glory, the phenomenal career, the fun, the joy, Del Mar, Santa Anita, the Eclipse Awards, the Kentucky Derby, beating rivals, breaking records ... in a flash, without warning, they were all yanked away. His agent at the time, Bob Meldahl, said, "Laffit was alive, and we were grateful, but a death had occurred and everyone knew it."

Laffit looked regal, Roseann remembers thinking, like an Aztec prince in his black crown when they went in to see him. Even in crippling pain, he held his head high. He was never without dignity.

His brother Juan joked that he looked more like a queen. The room broke into laughter. It helped.

Though it can be labeled a miracle that Laffit survived the fall, there's much to counter-balance the 'miracle' list.

Few wanted to acknowledge it at the time, but everyone came to believe it in the end:

If the ambulance people had stabilized Laffit,
If a real doctor was at the first aid center,
If he'd been taken directly to the hospital and x-rayed,
If doctors had spotted the breaks,
If they had put him into a halo immediately,
Then the opportunity for a real healing might have taken place.

Instead, because of the movement that took place between the time of the accident and the doctor putting on the halo, the bones jettisoned into more precarious positions, thereby making proper fusions impossible and because of that, Laffit lost any chance of ever being able to ride again.

In the end, his life was spared but because of the improper care, the very core of his life, the thing he lived to do most—his riding—was stolen from him.

It was a very bitter trade-off.

AFTER THE FALL

CHAPTER 28

The entire landscape of Laffit's life changed in the short amount of time he and Jeanine spent in the doctor's office. He'd entered thinking he was about to be released only to find out his sentence was commuted to life. Hopes and dreams—a life—were crushed that afternoon and what lay ahead was completely unknown.

Jeanine and Laffit rode home in silence, each trying to absorb what had just taken place. Jeanine was not surprised by the news, and though she thought she would be relieved, feeling her husband's overwhelming sadness tempered her relief.

Laffit was in shock. In the very back of his mind he *knew* he was going to ride again. There hadn't been a doubt during the past ten weeks. He had always, always rebounded. Pain did not dissuade him, nor did fear ever grip him. All he needed to do was endure, and endure he had these last few months, through the most difficult physical challenge of his life. He was more than willing to do so, just so he could get back on a horse and compete again.

And now it was over. Conversations lately with Jeanine and Lisa and Laffit III broached the topic of retirement, but Laffit quickly squelched the idea whenever the subject came up. There would be no retirement until *he* resolved the time was right. Now the decision was out of his hands.

Or was it? For a while, Laffit turned things over in his head. Clearly the doctor thought it was not wise to ride, that the chances for permanent paralysis were greatly increased, but a bigger question had to be answered.

What was his life about, Laffit asked himself, if not riding?

Though he loved his family dearly, his riding addiction was the most enduring relationship in his life. It had been the one constant his entire life. It preceded his children, it survived his first wife's death and without a doubt, it was the thing that saw him through grief, pain and financial ruin. It was the perfect sweet spot in his life. How on earth could he abandon those three minutes of joy when the rest of the world faded away and he rode through the heavens?

In truth, he couldn't. For Laffit, the reward was worth the risk. Life without riding just wouldn't be life.

The problem would be in telling Jeanine.

Through the past three months, Jeanine was as devoted as any wife could be. The accident hadn't happened just to him, it shook her to her core, too. The fall had also taken a toll on his children. Did he have a right to put them through this again? Or worse? What if he rode, had an accident, and wound up permanently paralyzed?

Bill Shoemaker's phone call helped make up his mind. Being Laffit's mentor placed The Shoe in a special position. Since his horrible accident, Shoemaker had been stoic in his endurance. No one heard one word of complaint about his being confined to a wheelchair. Until the day he called Laffit.

"Laffit, you don't want to risk this," Shoe said. "You don't. This is hell. You don't want to be in this position ever, trust me."

The warning pulled Laffit up short. He had obligations to the people who loved him. He couldn't just make decisions that might negatively affect them without considering them. The children were terrified but clearly, the person who would be most impacted would be Jeanine, the woman who'd stood so solidly behind him. She didn't deserve a life as a nursemaid.

And so, out of love for Jeanine, Laffit acquiesced. He would give up riding.

It was the hardest thing he'd ever done.

Laffit phoned Mike Mooney, the publicist at Hollywood Racetrack. Mike came from good horseracing stock and bore the love of the sport in his genes. Mike had been there over the years through countless races with Laffit and was there the day Laffit broke Shoemaker's record. Mike had become a friend over time, someone Laffit trusted and admired.

"Mike, I'm going to retire," Laffit announced to his friend. He heard the deep exhale on the other end of the phone. Before Mike could say anything Laffit continued. "I'd appreciate it if you'd write the announcement."

"It would be my honor," Mike replied.

Within an hour Mike had pounded out an announcement he'd anticipated having to write, but didn't want to do. When he read over what he'd written, Mike Mooney—a great lover of all things horse racing—broke down and cried. For Mike, it was the end of an era.

The announcement was made by Hollywood Park on April 29, 2003, during Kentucky Derby week.

An enormous retirement celebration was arranged for July 13. That day colleagues and friends spoke of Laffit's great dedication and talent. At the end of the tributes, Laffit, his hair just barely grown out since the removal of the surgical halo, spoke to the crowd.

"I want to thank my friends. I want to thank my fans and I want to thank Hollywood Park. This gives me an opportunity to say good-bye. I love you and I am standing here feeling very sad because I am leaving a sport I really love very much. I still have that fire in me that I cannot put out. I'm going to miss going out there every day, trying to win a race. I am very proud of my family," and with that Laffit had to stem the tears that began. He grabbed Jean-Laffit, hugged him close and then continued, "I am very proud to be a Panamanian and I am very proud to be living in this great country."

And then it was over.

For Laffit what came after was what he described as a "black hole that just opened up and swallowed me."

The months following were as bleak as any he'd ever encountered. Laffit didn't go to the track, couldn't even watch the races on television. Friends called, but Laffit was not in a social mood and declined all invitations. Jeanine seemed to be as saddened as Laffit. They spent their time at home watching movies on their big screen TV, trying to absorb the new order of their life. Jean-Laffit said, "We used to go to the track every weekend. Now there was nothing to do. It was strange."

"Want to go to Vegas for the week-end?" Laffit asked Jeanine.

"Not really. Do you want to go? I'll go if you want."

"Naw, I don't think so. Just thought you'd like to get away."

"I'm fine here," Jeanine told him.

"Me, too."

And so it went.

In retrospect, they both might have benefited from some counseling but neither felt the need. The depression that engulfed Laffit was all encompassing. It wasn't that he was denied a part of his identity, it felt as though he had lost *all* of it. If he wasn't a jockey, what was he? If he couldn't ride, what was his worth? If he couldn't win, where was the joy?

Because he couldn't talk about it, the questions fermented within him and turned him sour. He felt no pleasure anymore. In his head he still felt he had to keep himself in shape, to maintain his diet. It would take almost a year before he acknowledged that there was no need to diet as extremely, or exercise as vigorously but the habits of thirty-seven years don't die easily.

He also was aware of some small amount of resentment toward Jeanine. Though he understood his wife's fear of his riding again, it was because of her that he wasn't still on a horse. If he were unmarried, Laffit knew, he would be riding. At least, that's what ran around in his brain.

Slowly, things began to come back to life for Laffit. Since he finally had the time, Laffit decided he would do something he had wished to do for years—become an American citizen. He had begun the process a couple of times before but riding always got in the way.

Laffit wanted to become a citizen not only because he loved the United States but also because he felt he owed it a lot after all it had given him. Happily he could still retain his Panamanian citizenship; a country he still loves dearly. Jeanine was with him for the swearing-in ceremony, an event both moving and exciting for Laffit.

Shortly after, Laffit was approached by Jim Wilson for a second time. Wilson was still interested in producing a documentary DVD about Laffit's life. Wilson told Laffit that Kevin Costner would narrate. At this juncture, the timing was perfect and filming turned out to be great fun for Laffit.

When the film was completed, Wilson held a private screening of *All About Winning* during the summer season at Del Mar Racetrack to which Laffit invited a large contingent of family and friends. He and Jeanine sat in the middle of an outdoor screening room, especially constructed for the event, excited to see the film. Lisa and Laffit III and Jean-Laffit sat directly behind their dad and Jeanine.

The documentary is a rich, accurate film that chronicles Laffit's life and career. By necessity, everything is covered: Laffit's early life in Panama, his move to the United States, his early wins and naturally, his marriage to Linda.

During the screening, though everything started well, the atmosphere suddenly changed around the family. It was clear where the tension was coming from. Jeanine's back arched whenever Linda's photo graced the screen. First wife syndrome was rearing its ugly head. Though Jeanine was prominently featured in the film, Laffit could sense Jeanine's brittleness. Jeanine managed to be gracious to everyone when the film was over, but walking to the car she turned frigidly silent.

In the car, Laffit asked, "Are you okay?"

Jeanine turned on Laffit in a fury. "How could you let them do that to me?"

"What are you talking about?"

"They made Linda out to be a saint. I've been married to you as long as she has. How could you let them do that?"

"Jeanine, I had no say in the matter."

"But I'm your wife."

"Of course you are."

"Then why was she in this?"

"Because Linda was my wife as well."

"And they glorified her. All my friends were there. I was humiliated."

No matter what Laffit said to soothe her, Jeanine bristled. Years later, Laffit looked back and saw that that was the breaking point. Lisa and Laffit III said you could almost hear something snap that night as they sat behind Jeanine. Whatever the film meant to her, or how it affected her, was hard to pinpoint, but something got tapped that she was never able to get beyond.

Shortly thereafter Jeanine began dieting and exercising strenuously. She insisted on having her teeth fixed. She was, as Laffit saw later, preparing to leave.

The intimacy, the fun, the couple used to enjoy began to diminish. No matter how many times Laffit tried to assure Jeanine that Linda was his past and she was his present, it didn't help. She became intractable on the subject. The film should never have been made. It was a source of great pain and humiliation for her.

The vibes in the house grew cool. The couple that used to argue and make up easily became fierce in their disagreements. Jeanine began having dinners with girlfriends, something she'd never done before. She ran the track at the Rose Bowl and suddenly didn't want Laffit to join her, "You go too slow," she told him. The wife who was normally devoted and caring suddenly grew uninterested in anything Laffit said or did.

In bed one evening Jeanine told Laffit that she wasn't in love with him any longer. "And I don't think you love me anymore, either."

Laffit was stunned. "I *do* love you. I *am* in love with you. How can you say that?"

She thought they should separate for a while.

"I don't believe in separations," he told her.

He suggested they see a therapist. Laffit got the names of marriage counselors from Lisa. "Do you want to see a man or a woman? I have the names of both," he mentioned one morning.

"Jesus Christ, can't I wake up and have my tea before you hit me with this crap?"

From then on, tension rose in the formerly happy home.

Before he could recover from the first blow, things got worse. Jeanine wanted him to move out of the house.

"No," he replied, "you want this separation, you leave." And he prevailed. But Jeanine insisted on taking that which Laffit treasured most, their son Jean-Laffit. Laffit would not only lose his wife but his child as well.

The day Jeanine moved out, Laffit didn't want to be home. It would be too painful to see her leave. When he returned, the house felt desolate.

Jeanine told Laffit he needed to see a therapist so, hoping to prove his willingness to work things out, he began going. After weeks of begging, Jeanine finally paid a visit. She went once. It was evident to Laffit that her heart was not in to saving the marriage.

He asked if she wanted a divorce, hoping to hear that she didn't. She said no, let's give it some time. Laffit was relieved. But after months of her coolness, combined with her unwillingness to see a counselor, Laffit could see where things were heading. When he mentioned divorce again, hoping again to call her bluff, Jeanine told him, "I'm filing tomorrow. You don't need to."

Laffit was stung.

Sleeping became a challenge. A friend suggested a sleeping pill but it made things worse. He wanted to stay in bed all day and hide, but Laffit forced himself to get up each morning and head to the gym.

Friends were supportive, but confused by Jeanine's behavior. This was, after all, the woman who had been so devoted during his health crisis. She'd been the model wife, caring for her injured husband. What happened? What changed? Was it that the glamour was over? Was it a mid-life crisis?

Naturally Laffit was concerned there might be another man but without real proof—and certainly Jeanine was not owning up to anything—Laffit was stymied. All he knew was that after the DVD screening, Jeanine was a different woman. Strangely, it wasn't his retirement that had caused the breakup. It was the documentary.

Laffit discussed his situation with Roger Stein, a well-known radio sports commentator, a fan of Laffit's, and most importantly, a friend. Roger, as a caring observer, thought it was possible that Jeanine was seeing someone. He suggested Laffit hire an investigator. Laffit declined but unbeknownst to Laffit, Roger contacted a private investigator and had Jeanine followed. He did it out of genuine concern for Laffit.

At the point when Laffit grew desperate to know more, he asked Roger for the name of the private detective. Laffit hoped that the man could lay his fears to rest once and for all. He didn't know Roger had already given the man the go-ahead.

When Laffit phoned the man, he told Laffit, "Yes, Roger called already. I've got something I think you should take a look at."

The man arrived at the house the next afternoon with a videotape.

"Are you sure you want to see this?" the detective asked.

Laffit nodded and watched the man load the tape into the television.

And there it was: Jeanine meeting a shirtless jogger at the Rose Bowl. The man kissed Jeanine twice. Though he said he needed clarity, when Laffit had the proof right it front of him, it was crushing. He dissolved onto the couch crying.

When confronted, Jeanine told Laffit that the man was just someone who was after her, but when Laffit told her he had a tape, she was visibly shaken.

Having her move out was hard; knowing she was cheating was harder still.

There was bitter irony—some would say karma—to what was happening to Laffit. All the times he'd cheated on Linda, even cheated on Phyllis with Jeanine; now when he'd been completely faithful to this wife, she had cheated on him.

It wasn't that he'd been unaware of other women during this relationship, or that women were no longer coming on to him. But in the thirteen years he'd been with Jeanine, he never cheated. Ever.

During their separation when he confessed his pain and loneliness to Jeanine, she would grow scornful. He begged for them to stay together for the sake of their son. At one point, she relented saying maybe they should try. But even when she said it, Laffit worried. Though he was anxious to believe that it could work, could he really forget?

The reconciliation didn't last long. Neither of them seemed to have the heart for it. Laffit worried about the effect all this was having on their son. He tried his best to be upbeat when he saw Jean-Laffit, but knew he wasn't fooling him.

The daily struggles proved daunting. On his own for the first time in his life, Laffit discovered that he didn't know even the simplest of things: how to open a checking account; how to set up a fax machine; in short, how to take care of himself. He was a man who had always been cared for by women, spoiled by them, and suddenly he was thrust into a world of self-reliance. In the beginning it terrified him. If it hadn't been for Roger, he'd have been lost. Roger's help and counsel saw him through.

Other friends were a comfort. They took him to dinner, listened to his troubles and offered what support they could. But at night, he returned to an empty house and slept in an empty bed and tried to figure out what had gone wrong. She was too young, perhaps when they married. She hadn't had a chance to date a lot of different men. She was thirty-five years-old now. Maybe just being a housewife wasn't enough anymore. He understood those things. They gave him some comfort but the real reason she left was still elusive.

He heard through friends that Jeanine was seen around town with the man in the video. Each spotting was a knife in the heart.

Tom Kessler, a businessman and horse owner, only knew Laffit slightly prior to this time, but proved to be a new and invaluable friend. Tom connected to Laffit because he knew what it was like to be lonely. Tom himself had lost a beloved wife to cancer some years earlier. At a time when Laffit was most vulnerable, it was Tom who assured him that he would surmount this crisis just as he had so many others.

Tom, a father himself who was sensitive regarding children, stepped in and was instrumental in making things as fun for Jean-Laffit as possible when Laffit was not able to do so himself. Tom invited the two to baseball games, took them fishing, out to movies, and to dinner. Tom's laughter and light-heartedness slowly helped heal some of the pain both Laffit and his son were experiencing.

Tom also had dinners privately with Laffit and reminded him of who he was and that he would recover. More than anything, Tom believed that Laffit was a winner, even if he didn't feel like one at the time.

Before long, Tom's ministerings began to work. The two bachelors were seen with pretty young woman at their favorite restaurants: Bistro 45, The Derby and Shogun. Eventually there was even some laughter at those dinners.

Though the empty house was seemingly impossible to adjust to at first, over the coming months Laffit began to appreciate the simplicity of his life. He no longer had to ask permission to go anywhere. He could spend what he liked, do what he pleased, eat when it suited him. For the first time in his entire life, Laffit was completely self-reliant. And he liked it!

He had the tattoo on his arm with Jeanine's name covered over with a black panther.

A trip to Panama with Tom Kessler in January of 2007 was uplifting. Tom said, "Going to Panama with Laffit is like going to London with John Lennon." Wined and dined by local dignitaries, Laffit was reinvigorated by his Panamanian roots.

At a baseball game they attended, Tom recalls a young boy spotting Laffit below him in the grandstand. The boy yelled, "Laffit," and when Laffit turned, the boy tossed his ball cap down to him. "Sign it, please," the boy shouted. Laffit did and tossed the hat back up. When the others in the stands saw what happened, a hundred baseball caps came raining down on Laffit. He signed every single one before leaving. Laffit's smile was more relaxed when he left the ball park that day.

Attracting women was never a problem for Laffit and when friends knew he was ready, they each had multiple females lined up to vie for his attentions. Like a young boy released in a candy shop, Laffit enjoyed spending time with a variety of women. He began to feel alive again.

The divorce grew complicated, then straight-forward, then messy again. A settlement was finally reached on June 7, 2007. Both parties would move forward.

As Laffit learned how to take care of himself, both physically and emotionally, his energies began to soar. The lawsuit against the ambulance company that had failed to treat him properly when he broke his neck resulted in him being awarded $2.7 million.

The lawsuit against the man who misused his finances continues to bounce through the courts.

The cost of the divorce, the misuse of his funds by his financial planner, and his inability to ride any longer, has been challenging. Nonetheless, Laffit is grateful for all he has. And it is a lot.

With brothers Juan (left), Laffit, sister Margie, and Alonso (right).

NOW

CHAPTER 29

Laffit was packing. The big race was coming up and everyone was anxious to see him, but this time the spotlight was not focused on Laffit, it was on Russell Baze. It was Baze who was suddenly hot on the heels of Laffit's record of Winningest Jockey of All Time. What others thought would never be topped, was now close to being matched. Laffit drove to the airport to fly to San Francisco. He would be there to congratulate the man when he overtook his record.

To many in the horseracing world, Baze's record—though admirable—was not considered in the same league as Laffit's. Jim Altfeld, who worked at Santa Anita, voiced what many people felt. "Baze is not even fit to breath the same air as Laffit ... and Russsell knows it. Russell is basically a Golden Gate, Northern California rider. It's not the same caliber of horse. He's also not competing against the other real riders. He's a big fish in a small pond. He didn't compete against great jockeys. Laffit competed against Shoe, Baeza, Cordero, McCarron, Delahoussaye, Stevens. He went up against Hall of Fame jockeys and flew all over the country in all the great races. Baze didn't do that."

But none of that mattered to Laffit. He admired Baze and would congratulate him when the time came. Twice he flew to Bay Meadows hoping Baze would make it, sitting through every race of the day. Finally, on December 1, 2006, Baze succeeded on a horse named Butterfly Belle. Laffit was gracious in his praise of Baze. Though he had hoped to retain the record for some years, he was sincere in his admiration of Baze's achievement. He had, after all, learned from the best. Like Shoemaker, Laffit felt it important to be there to pass on the torch. He told reporters.

"Russell is a great rider," Pincay said. "He works very hard out there every day. It takes a lot of ability and a lot of dedication. He deserves the record."[31]

In kind, Baze praised Laffit. "I'd like to thank Laffit for being here. I knew I had one person pulling for me. There's

---

[31] "Baze Gets All-Time Wins Mark," Chuck Dybdal, *Daily Racing Form*, December 1, 2006.

not a greater rider or better sportsman in horse racing than Laffit."[32]

Laffit's legacy is not merely that he was a great rider, he is someone who helped transform the sport so men like Russell Baze could ride more safely. Initially, Laffit was reluctant to sue the ambulance company that served Santa Anita Racetrack, but after talking to many jockeys he realized that the only way change would take place would be if there was real incentive—in the form of financial penalties—for not doing the sensible thing. From now on, at every racetrack in the United States, when a jockey is thrown from a horse, he is taken directly by ambulance to an area hospital where the injured jockey can be examined by medical personnel. No other jockey will ever walk around for five days with a broken neck—and destroy his career—and not know it.

If a man is measured by the regard in which he is held by those closest to him, than Laffit ranks as a king among men.

It is easy for strangers to see the triumph of a talented man and be enraptured. It's quite another thing to have long-term friendships, many lasting forty years or more, in which people still refer to the man as "perfect," "god-like," "superior," "remarkable," "gifted," "blessed," "generous," "super-human"—all words used to describe Laffit. When people in your business think you define the sport, it is significant.

---

[32] Ibid.

"The man is our Cal Ripken (baseball), Wayne Gretzky (hockey), Michael Jordan (basketball) rolled into 117 powerful Panamanian pounds," said Richard Eng, in the *Las Vegas Review-Journal*.

Speak to any of the people from Laffit's inner circle and they all describe the times when he rode as magical, and Laffit a rare and gifted athlete.

Laffit with bust commemorating him as all time leading jockey at Santa Anita.

"He was the most dedicated rider I ever met in my life," said Angel Cordero, himself a remarkable rider and winner of three Kentucky Derbys.

"He continuously sacrificed for forty years! Forty years, every day! No athlete could do that today," said Vince DeGregory, his former agent.

What both men were referring to was the unwavering focus on racing that Laffit displayed. While many jockeys can toe the line for five to seven years, none has ever had to sacrifice so much for so long. And that is only part of what sets the man apart.

Angel Cordero said, "He was making hundreds of thousands of dollars a year, but the man couldn't even have a steak at the end of a long day of racing. It's like being thirsty and not being able to have a sip of water. Nobody could do that now. I never saw anyone pull weight [lose weight quickly] and accomplish what he did."

DeGregory went on, "Laffit was the cleanest rider ever. He would frustrate other riders because he could win naturally. Others would be whipping their horses in the last quarter mile and Laffit would throw his crop away and just carry the horse to win, naturally, with his strength. That's what made him the great rider that he was."

His last agent, Bob Meldahl said, "The greatest athletes—there's an air about them. To see his dedication and Laffit's will to be the best; I've never seen it in any other athlete."

The loyalties and affections Laffit engenders can also be heart breaking. DeGregory, the agent who helped propel Laffit to superstar status, but also drove the jockey harder than he could handle, says his heart broke when the partnership ended after so many great years together. Speaking to him today, one senses that those were the "good old days," the days of glory, extraordinary glory, that have never been matched. "There was a magic," he said, "in the partnership." It is almost as though he never recovered.

Bob Meldahl said his heart was broken when Laffit took his terrible fall that afternoon at Santa Anita. While certainly there was concern about business—Meldahl being his agent at the time—it was secondary to his deep concerns about Laffit the person. (Let's face it, any agent who has handled Laffit Pincay Jr. will not have trouble finding another jockey to represent.) But the loss for Meldahl took something out of him—"the heart"—he declared. Ironically, within a year of Laffit's unexpected retirement, Meldahl underwent open-heart surgery. And Laffit was there to offer encouragement during his recovery.

Two men's hearts affected by one remarkable jockey. DeGregory's broken by the loss, Meldahl's damaged, but fixed.

It would appear that loving Laffit can be a costly business.

EPILOGUE

W e have sat in Laffit's elegant den, surrounded by paintings of jockeys on horseback and various riding awards for nearly two years now. Our routine is familiar but today, out of the blue, Laffit announces "I've been wanting to tell you something."

He begins in a voice that is gentler than usual, yet there is a kind of urgency in his tone. "When I was racing, I used to challenge myself all the time," he starts. "Some days I would drive myself to the track and I would be deathly ill. I would have been up all night, or I'd have a fever or a broken ankle that I didn't know how I was going to stuff into my boots. Sometimes, my mind was wrapped up with whatever was bothering me emotionally. Whatever it was, there was always something that was a completely legitimate excuse to turn the car around and go back home and get back into bed. I could have called my agent or a trainer and explained things and they would have understood. But I didn't. Instead, I used those things to challenge myself.

"I know I have a migraine headache, but let's see if I can still ride."

"Sure I have a temperature of 102, but I wonder if I can win anyway."

"My wife may be hospitalized, but I want to see what I can do today."

Whatever the problem, Laffit chose to view it as a challenge. It was he, and he alone, who set the bar to the heavens. It was never, as I had occasionally thought, what anyone else said to him, it was what he said to himself that made him surmount each obstacle that came his way. The obstacles changed from physical to emotional, from external to internal, and back again. Sometimes more than one obstacle had to be faced at the same time, doubling the demands he placed on himself.

Over the years, Laffit had seen many jockeys who fell under the pressures and collapsed. To be riding day after day, to be risking your life for unknown amounts of money, to have to deal with a personal life at the same time, is often what separates the ultimate winners from the losers. Not everyone is capable of the single-mindedness of purpose that Laffit displayed.

I was curious how Laffit could take what was debilitating and turn it into a challenge.

"So you just made yourself ride?"

"No, I made it a challenge. I made it a game almost."

"And how did you feel if you did well on one of those days when you didn't want to ride? " I asked.

"Oh, I felt just great!"

"And if you lost?"

"Then I said to myself, well at least you tried. Either way, I felt good about myself."

Ah, the creation of true self-esteem.

This story, I realized, more than any others, summarized Laffit's philosophy of life, of winning. His motivation came not from other jockeys, or from his agent, or from a loved one but from within, which was the reason he was able to stay on top for so very long.

Laffit's story of success is not limited to the riding world. It is an example for all of us who are occasionally tempted to call in sick, to use legitimate excuses for not getting something done, for not facing an unpleasant situation, for avoiding whatever's bothering us.

If anyone faced horrendous obstacles in his life and overcame them, it has been Laffit. Knowing the man now I can say that there is certainly some rare spark within him that few possess. But there is also a very human being who forced himself to get up on mornings when he didn't want to face the world, the mornings after Linda died, the days when the FBI was dogging him, the days and nights when he was in pain, the weeks following Jeanine leaving him. Laffit not only faced his fears, he conquered them by sheer force of will, by determination and by constantly challenging himself.

That day Laffit defined for me what the anatomy of a winner is.

It's him.

Laffit today

APPENDIX

UPDATE

Here's where some of the people in Laffit's life are now:

- His mother Rosario, age eighty-four, lives in her own home in Arcadia. She is mentally very sharp. Her son visits her every day.
- His sister Margie and her husband Cesar, both retired, split their time between Panama and Arcadia.
- His stepbrother Juan works for Southwest Airlines and lives in Maryland.
- His stepbrother Alonso lives in Los Angeles and works at the tracks.
- His daughter Lisa is happily married to husband David and has two children, Madelyn (Maddy) and Mason.
- Laffit Pincay III lives in Pasadena, is single, and works as an announcer for HRTV. He is still friends with his childhood buddy Ian.

- Jean-Laffit is now a sophomore in high school.
- Humberto Aguilera lives in Los Angeles and is an entrepreneur.
- Roseann is a realtor in Beverly Hills who still loves going to the track and is close to Lisa and Young Laffit and Lisa's children.
- Millie now lives in Los Angeles and is also very involved in her niece's and nephew's lives. She, too, is a realtor.
- Cindy Shoemaker lives in Palm Desert, California, and is a landscape designer.
- Roger Stein is still a close friend of Laffit's. He trains horses and has his own radio show.
- Angel Cordero is retired and lives in New York.
- Vince DeGregory is currently agent to jockey Joel Rosario.
- Bob Meldahl is agent to two jockeys, Julio Garcia and Isais Enriquez.
- Mike Mooney is still the publicist at Hollywood Racetrack.
- Phyllis Davis lives in Arizona. She and Laffit have renewed their friendship.
- Marge Everett is retired and lives in Beverly Hills.
- Tom Kessler still owns horses and remains Laffit's close friend.
- Camillo Marin and Dr. Robert Kerlan are both deceased.

DIET FOR LIFE

Since his retirement, many anticipated that Laffit would finally indulge in all the foods he denied himself for years. Though he allows himself a bit more leeway, his diet is still health conscious and his physique, remarkably trim.

Many have asked what his secret is. Here is what Laffit eats these days:

BREAKFAST

2 ounces of a baked yam (including skin) or 1 small apple (with skin)

1 teaspoon Fat Free Cool Whip or 1 teaspoon French Deluxe Vanilla Non Diary Creamer

6 ounces water

8 drops of Stevia (a sweetener from the health food store)

1 packet Wheatgrass Powder (by Easy Pha-Max)*

2 teaspoons of Citrucel fiber

Use a hand blender or a mixer to thoroughly blend.

LUNCH

½ cup steamed organic broccoli florets

½ cup steamed green beans (both of these are topped with 'I Can't Believe It's Not Butter Spray)

2-3 ounces of protein (chicken, fish or beef) cooked without oil or butter

1 Kavli 5 grain Crispbread

DINNER

The same as lunch though he increases his intake to 3 to 4 ounces of protein.

If he consumes alcohol he prefers vodka because it is considered purer but he will occasionally have a glass of red wine (which he sweetens with Splenda.)

Twice a day Laffit makes Ginseng Tea and puts a packet of Wheatgrass Powder into it.

* Easy Pha-Max powder can be obtained at www.laffitpincayjr.com

EXERCISE

Certainly years of exercise has helped keep Laffit in great shape. Currently he exercises six days a week for an hour each day. He walks on the treadmill for 45 minutes and lifts 30-50 pounds for 15 minutes.

Come rain or shine.

LAFFIT PINCAY JR.'S
CAREER RECORD*

1964-2003

Triple Crown Wins
>Kentucky Derby (GI-CD)
>>Swale (1984)
>Belmont S. (GI-Bel)
>>Conquistador Cielo (1982)
>>Caveat (1983)
>>Swale (1984)

Breeders' Cup Wins
>Classic (GI)
>>Skywalker (1986-SA)

Distaff (GI)
> Bayakoa (1989-GP, 1990-Bel)

Juvenile (GI)
> Tasso (1985-Aqu)
> Capote (1986-SA)
> Is It True (1988-CD)

Juvenile Fillies (GI)
> Phone Chatter (1993-SA)

Million Dollar Wins

Arlington Million (GI–AP)
> Perrault (NG-1982)
> Tight Spot (1991)

Breeders' Cup Classic (GI)
> Skywalker (1986-SA)

Breeders' Cup Distaff (GI)
> Bayakoa (1989-GP,1990-Bel)

Breeders' Cup Juvenile (GI)
> Tasso (1985-Aqu)
> Capote (1986-SA)
> Is It True (1988-CD)

Breeders' Cup Juvenile Fillies (GI)
> Phone Chatter (1993-SA)

Hollywood Futurity (GI-Hol)
Tejano (1987)

Jersey Derby (GIII-GS)
Spend A Buck (1985)

Jockey Club Gold Cup (GI-Bel)
Crème Fraiche (1987)

Santa Anita Handicap (GI-SA)
Greignton (1986)

Major Stakes Wins

Affirmed H. (GIII-Hol)
Valdez (GII-1979)
Tights (GII-1984)
Pancho Villa (GII-1985)
Stalwart Charger (1990)
Natural Nine (1992)

American H. (GII-Hol)
Figonero (NG-1969)
Plunk (1974)
Effervescing (1978)
Clever Song (1987)
Tight Spot (1991)

Arcadia H. (GII-SA)
> Lazy Lode (2001)

Arlington Million (GI-AP)
> Perrault (NG-1982)
> Tight Spot (1991)

BelAir H. (GII-Hol)
> What Goes On (NG-1971)
> Tri Jet (NG-1973)
> Sirlad (NG-1979)
> Super Diamond (GIII-1986)
> Smile Again (2001)

Beldame (GI-Bel)
> Gamely H. (NG-1968-1969)
> Susan's Girl (NG-1972)
> Desert Vixen (1974)

Belmont S. (GI-Bel)
> Conquistador Cielo (1982)
> Caveat (1983)
> Swale (1984)

Beverly Hills H. (GI-Hol)
> Manta (NG-1971)
> Bastonera II (GII-1976)
> Country Queen (GIII-1980)

Virginie (1999)

Breeders' Cup Classic (GI)
Skywalker (1986-SA)

Breeders' Cup Distaff (GI)
Bayakoa (1989-GP; 1990-Bel)

Breeders' Cup Juvenile (GI)
Tasso (1985-Aqu)
Capote (1986-SA)
Is It True (1988-CD)

Breeders Cup Juvenile Fillies (GI)
Phone Chatter (1993-SA)

Buena Vista S. (GII-SA)
Rare Charmer (2001)

Cal Fed Snow Chief S. (Hol)
Calkins Road (2002)

California Cup Classic (OT)
College Town (1994)
Sky Jack (2000)
Calkins Road (2002)

Californian (GI-Hol)

Ancient Title (1975)
Crystal Water (1977)
Affirmed (1979)
Erins Isle (1982)
Greignton (1985)

Charles Whittingham Memorial H (GI-Hol)
Life Cycle (1973)
John Henry (1981)
Exploded (1982)
Erins Isle (1983)
Steinlen (1990)

Cigar Mile H. (GI-Aqu)
Ibero (1992)

Cinema H. (GIII-Hol)
Pinjara (NG-1968)
Noholme Jr. (NG-1969)
D'Artagnan (NG-1970)
Finalista (NG-1972)
Bad N'Big (GII-1977)
Something Lucky (GII-1987)
Sligo Bay (2001)

Citation H. (GII-Hol)
Effervescing (1978)
Notorious Pleasure (1991, 1st div)

Fly Till Dawn (1991, 2nd div)

Del Mar Derby (GII-Dmr)
    Relaunch (GIII-1979)
    Exploded (GIII-1980)
    Give Me Strength (1982)
    Tight Spot ((1990)
    Ocean Crest (1994)

Del Mar Futurity (GII-Dmr)
    Visible (1976)
    Althea (1983)
    Tasso (GI-1985)
    Lost Kitty (GI-1987)

Del Mar H. (GII-Dmr)
    Royal Chariot (1995)
    Timboroa (2001)

Del Mar Oaks (GII-Dmr)
    Go Much (GIII-1976)
    Heartlight No. One (1983)

Desert Stormer H. (GII-Hol)
    Slewsbox (2002)

Eddie Read H. (GI-Dmr)
    Effervescing (NG-1978)

Ten Below (GII-1984)
Sharrood (GII-1987)
Tight Spot (1991)

Florida Derby (GI-GP)
Judger (1974)
Swale (1984)

Frank E Kilroe Mile H. (GII-SA)
Royal Dynasty (NG-1970)
Exceller (GIII-1978)
Fluorescent Light (GIII-1979)
Premier Minister (GIII-1981)
Perrault (GIII-1982)
Fly Till Dawn (GIII-1992)
College Town (1995)
Road to Slew (2001)

Frizette S. (GI-Bel)
Molly Ballantine (1974)
Heavenly Cause ((1980)
Family Style (1985)
Some Romance (1988)

Futurity (GI-Bel)
Spectacular Love (1984)

Gamely H. (GI-Hol)

Rising Market (NG-1968)
Katonka (NG-1976)
Ack's Secret (GII-1982)
Miss Josh (1991)

Gazelle H. (Bel)
Susan's Girl (1972)

Goodwood H. (GIII-OT)
Super Diamond (1986)

Haskell Invitational H. (GI-Mth)
Forty Niner (1988)

Hawthorne Derby (GIII-Haw)
Hymn-DH (2000)

Hawthorne H. (GII-Hol)
Tallahto (NG-1974)
Sensational (NG-1978)
Country Queen (NG-1979-80)
Adored (1985)
Dontstop Themusic (1986)
Bayakoa (1989-90)

Hollywood Derby (Hol)
Bold Reason (1971)

Hollywood Futurity (GI-Hol)
>Tejano (1987)
>River Special (1992)
>Valiant Nature (1993)
>Tactical Cat (1998)

Hollywood Gold Cup (GI-Hol)
>Pleasure Seeker (NG-1970)
>Ancient Title (1975)
>Crystal Water (1977)
>Affirmed (1979)
>Perrault (1982)
>Grienton (1985)
>Super Diamond (1986)
>Aptitude (2001)
>Sky Jack (2002)

Hollywood Juvenile Championship (GIII-Hol)
>Insubordination (NG-1969)
>Dimaggio (GII-1974)
>Affirmed (GII-1977)
>Loma Malad (GII-1980)
>The Captain (GII-1981)
>Althea (GII-1983)
>Squirtle Squirt (2000)

Hollywood Oaks (GI-Hol)
>Miss Musket (GII-1974)

Tango Dancer (1982)
Heartlight No. One (1983)

Hollywood Prevue S. (GIII-Hol)
Fonz's (2001)

Hollywood Starlet (GII-Hol)
Althea (1983)

Hollywood Turf Cup (GI-Hol)
Lazy Lode (1999)
Sligo Bay (2002)

Honeymoon H. (GIII-Hol)
Le Cle (NG-1972) *
Katonka (NG-1975)
Joyous Ways (1977)

Inglewood H. (GII-Hol)
Rising Market (NG-1969)
Star Spangled (NG-1979)
Tight Spot (1991)

Jersey Derby (GIII-GS)
Spend A Buck (1985)

Jim Murray Memorial H. (Hol)
Mashaallah (1994)

Jockey Club Gold Cup (GI-Bel)
   Affirmed (1979)
   Crème Fraiche (1987)

Kentucky Derby (GI-CD)
   Swale (1984)

Kentucky Oaks (GI-CD)
   Heavenly Cause (1981)

La Canada S. (GII-SA)
   Hollywood Glitter (GI-1988)
   Exchange (1992)

Landluce S. (GIII-Hol)
   Consider Me Lucky (NG-1969)
   Special Goddess (1973)
   Wavy Waves (1976)
   Native Fancy (1980)
   Landaluce (1982)

Las Flores H. (GIII-SA)
   Everything Lovely (NG-1970)
   Matching (NG-1983)
   Foggy Nation (1985)
   Very Subtle (1989)
   Enjoy the Moment (1999)

Los Angeles H. (GIII-Hol)
>   Rising Market (NG-1968)
>   Ancient Title (GII-1974)
>   Big Band (GII-1975)
>   Beau's Eagle (1980)
>   Sam Who (1989)
>   Men's Exclusive (1997)

Matriarch (GI-Hol)
>   Kilijaro (NG-1981)
>   Exchange (1994)

Matron (GI-Bel)
>   Fiesta Lady (1984)

Meadowlands Cup (GI-Med)
>   Crème Fraiche (1987)

Mervyn LeRoy H. (GII-Hol)
>   Skywalker (1986)
>   Zabaleta (1987)
>   Ruhlmann (GI-1989)
>   Sky Jack (2002)

Metropolitan Mile H. (GI-Bel)
>   Czaravich (1980)
>   Ibero (1993)

Milady Br. Cup H. (GI-Hol)
    Princessnesian (NG-1968)
    Desert Law (NG-1969)
    Bastonera II (GII-1976)
    Adored (GII-1984-85)
    Bayakoa (1989-90)

Monrovia H. (GIII-SA)
    Little Happiness (NG-1978)
    Lil Sister Stich (2002)

Native Diver H. (GIII-Hol)
    Life's Hope (1979)
    Hopeful Word (1986)
    Sky Jack (2000)
    Piensa Sonando (2002)

Norfolk S. (GI-OT)
    Capote (1986)

Oak Leaf S. (GI-OT)
    Landaluce (1982)
    Folk Art (1984)
    Phone Chatter (1993)
    Tipically Irish (1995)

Oak Tree Turf Ch. (GI-OT)

Tallahto (1974)
John Henry (1980)

Palos Verdes H. (GII-SA)
Rising Market (NG-1968)
Ancient Title (NG-1974)
Maheras (NG-1976)
Chinook Pass (NG-1982)
Phone Trick (NG-1985)
Individualist (GIII-1992)
Men's Exclusive (2001)

Philip H. Iselin H. (GI-Mth)
Spend A Buck (1985)

Princess S. (GIII-Hol)
Le Cle (NG-1972)
Gene's Lady (1984)
Melair (1986)

Railbird S. (GII-Hol)
Impressive Style (NG-1972)
Sheesham (1988)

Ramona H. (GIII-Dmr)
Country Queen (1979)

Ruffian H. (GI-Bel)

It's In the Air (1979)
Heartlight No. One (1983)
Bayakoa (1989)

San Felipe S. (GII-SA)
Unconscious (NG-1971)
Solar Salute (NG-1972)
Image of Greatness (GI-1985)
Medaglia d'Oro (2002)

San Juan Capistrano H. (GI-SA)
Practicante (NG-1972)
Erins Isle (1983)
Load the Cannons (1984)
Rosedale (1987)

Santa Anita Derby (GI-SA)
Alley Fighter (NG-1968)
Solar Salute (NG-1972)
Sham (1973)
An Act (1976)
Affirmed (1978)
Muttering (1982)
Skywalker (1985)

Santa Anita Handicap (GI-SA)
Cougar II (1973)
Crystal Water (1977)

Affirmed (1979)

John Henry (1981)

Greignton (1986)

Santa Anita Oaks (GI-SA)

Allie's Serenade (NG-1968)

Belle Marie (GII-1973)

Althea (1984)

Santa Barbara H. (GI-SA)

Princessneian (NG-1968, 2nd div)

Manta (NG-1971)

Susan's Girl (1973)

Tallahto (1974)

Kittyluck (1978)

Sisterhood (1980)

Ack's Secret (1982)

Exchange (1993)

Santa Margarita H. (GI-SA)

Miss Moona (NG-1967)

Manta (NG-1971)

Susan's Girl (1973)

Princess Karenda (1981)

Ack's Secret (1982)

Bayakoa (1989)

Senorita S. (GII-Hol)

Impressive Style (NG-1972)
Heartlight (NG-1984)
Rabiadella (1994)

Sorrento (GII-Dmr)
Telferner (NG-1976)
Native Fancy (NG-1980)
Cheval Volant (GIII-1989)
Phone Chatter (GIII-1993)
Give Praise (2000)

Strub S. (GI-SA)
Drin (NG-1967)
Snow Sporting (NG-1970)
Ancient Title (1974)
Affirmed (1979)
Diazo (1994)

Super Derby (GI-LaD)
Island Whirl (NG-1981)
Sunny's Halo (1983)
Gate Dancer (1984)

Swaps S. (GI-Hol)
Valdez (1979)
Noble Nashua (1981)
Devoted Brass (1993)

Three Chimney's Spinster (GI-Kee)
  Numbered Account (NG-1972)
  Susan's Girl (1975)
  Dontstop Themusic (1985)
  Bayakoa (1989-90)

Toyota Blue Grass S. (GI-Kee)
  Judger (GII-1974)
  Millennium Wind (2001)

Travers S. (GI-Sar)
  Bold Reason (NG-1971)
  Carr De Naskra (1984)

Triple Bend Br. Cup H. (GIII-Hol)
  Woodlands Pines (NG-1974)
  Fifty Six Ina Row (NG-1985)
  Robyn Dancer (1991)

Vanity H. (GI-Hol)
  Desert Law (NG-1969)
  Tallahto (1974)
  It's In the Air (1980)
  Bayakoa (1989)

Vernon O. Underwood (GIII-Hol)
  Pancho Villa (1985)
  Men's Exclusive (2000-01)

Vinery Del Mar Debutante (GI-Dmr)
>   Telferner (1976)
>   Landaluce (1982)
>   Althea (1983)
>   Fiesta Lady (1984)

Whitney H. (GII-Sar)
>   Tri Jet (1974)

Will Rogers H. (GII-Hol)
>   Poleax (NG-1968)
>   Fast Fellow (NG-1971)
>   Madera Sun (GIII-1976)
>   Tsunami Slew (GIII-1984)
>   Something Lucky (GIII-1987)
>   Notorious Pleasure (1989)

Woodward S. (GI-Bel)
>   Affirmed (1979)

Yellow Ribbon S. (GI-OT)
>   Country Queen (1979)

RECORDS

- Only six-time Eclipse Award winning jockey, trainer or owner.
- Awarded special Eclipse in 1999 for "Singular Achievement" of breaking Bill Shoemaker's record total of 8,833 victories.
- All-time leader in races won at Hollywood Park, Santa Anita and Del Mar.
- Won Santa Anita-record five stakes on October 28, 2000, Oak Tree California Cup Day, including the $250,000 Cal Cup Classic. His victory aboard Chichim in the Cal Cup Distaff placed him at the unprecedented 9,000-win plateau.

MILESTONES

- 9,500th win: January 30, 2003 on Saxony at Santa Anita.
- 9,000th win: October 28, 2000 on Chichim at Santa Anita.
- 8,834th win (breaks Shoemaker's record): December 10th, 1999 on Irish Nip at Hollywood Park.
- 8,883rd win (ties Shoemaker's record): December 9, 1999 on I Be Casual at Hollywood Park.
- Surpasses Bill Shoemaker to become the leading rider in track history at both Santa Anita and Hollywood Park in 1992. Becomes Del Mar's all-time leading rider in 1998.

RIDING TITLES

- Hollywood Park: 16 titles, most recently 2001 spring/summer. First was in 1968.
- Santa Anita: 14 titles, most recently in 2001. First was in 1969-70.
- Oak Tree: 1976, 1978, 1982, 2000, 2001, 2002.
- Del Mar: 1976, 1977, 1979, 1982,1985.
- Saratoga: 1971.
- Arlington Park: 1967.
- Hawthorne: 1968.

ACCOLADES

- Inducted into racing's Hall of Fame in 1975.
- Eclipse Awards in 1971, 1973, 1974, 1979, 1985, 1999 ("Singular achievement of breaking Bill Shoemaker's record total of 8,833 victories on December 10, 1999).
- George Woolf Memorial Jockey Award, 1970.
- Big Sport of Turfdom Award (only dual winner) from Turf Publicists of America, 1985 & 2000.
- Mike Venezia Memorial Award, 1996.
- Mervyn LeRoy Racing and Entertainment Award, 1997.

U.S. RIDING RECORD

1966-2003:   48,487 Mounts   9,530 Wins
$237,417,045 Earnings

* Hollywood Park 2003 Media Guide.

Legend of Abbreviations

Hol	Hollywood Park
SA	Santa Anita Racetrack
AP	Arlington Park
Bel	Belmont
GP	Gulfstream Park
AQU	Aqueduct
CD	Churchill Downs
OT	Oak Tree
DMR	Del Mar
KEE	Keeneland
MTH	Monmouth
HAW	Hawthorne
GS	Garden State Park
MED	Meadowlands
LAD	Louisiana Downs
SAR	Saratoga

Stakes Races

NG – Not graded; GI; GII; GIII